PAIN – THE UNEXPECTED GIFT

DOUG MCALLISTER

PAIN – THE UNEXPECTED GIFT
Copyright ©2016 by Doug McAllister

Unless otherwise noted, all Scripture quotations are taken from the Holy Bible, New King James Version. Copyright © 1982 by Thomas Nelson, Inc., Nashville, TN. Used by permission.

Scripture quotations marked KJV are taken from the Holy Bible, King James Version.

Scripture quotations marked MSG are taken from the Holy Bible, the Message translation. Copyright © 1993, 2002 by Eugene H. Peterson. Used by permission.

Scripture quotations marked NIV are taken from the Holy Bible, New International Version. Copyright © 1973, 1984, 2011 by Biblica, Inc. Used by permission.

Scripture quotations marked NLT are taken from the Holy Bible, New Living Translation. Copyright © 1996, 2013 by Tyndale House Foundation. Used by permission.

All rights reserved. No part of this publication may be reproduced, stored in a retrieval system, or transmitted in any form by means electronic, mechanical, photocopying, recording or otherwise, except for the inclusion of brief quotations in a review, without prior permission in writing from the publisher.

ISBN: 978-1-939779-44-1

Published by

LIFEBRIDGE
BOOKS
P.O. BOX 49428
CHARLOTTE, NC 28277

Dedication

*This is for you, Mom and Pop.
Thanks for your steadfast love through
the years and for ice cream
every Thursday night.*

Contents

Introduction		7
1	The Unexpected Gift	9
2	The Purpose of Pain	27
3	The Process of Pain	45
4	The Pain of Poverty	61
5	The Pain of Betrayal	79
6	The Pain of Family	97
7	The Pain of Discipline	109
8	The Pain of Change	125
9	The Pain of Emotion	139
10	Good Grief!	151

INTRODUCTION

It doesn't sound logical to associate a cruise on an ocean liner with pain and suffering, but I found myself experiencing just that.

My wife, Rachel, and I were privileged to travel with the international Christian relief agency, Convoy of Hope, on a summer cruise to Alaska. Oh, there were majestic sights along the way, but the purpose of our group was to strategize how best to serve people who are going through crises around the world.

The pressing needs we discussed with ministry leaders were heart-wrenching, especially the stories of men, women, and children who were faced with the ravages of war, drought, disease, natural disasters, and so much more.

I had many questions, most of them starting with the word, "Why?"

Then late one evening I walked out on one of the decks, watching the waters swirl by, when something unusual took place. It was as if the Holy Spirit invaded my quiet time and I had a visitation from Jesus. What He spoke to my heart was the impetus for what you are about to read on these pages.

The Lord showed me people who were desperate and hurting, but at the same time they were being given a gift from heaven itself. I saw the Lord at work in ways that were far different than we expect.

You are about to discover that regardless of the suffering or hardship you may be going through—or have endured in the past—there is an ultimate purpose behind it all.

From this day forward, I am praying that you will not view your problems as punishment, but instead will understand the favor and blessing of *Pain – The Unexpected Gift!*

– Doug McAllister

CHAPTER 1

EXPECT THE UNEXPECTED

You don't have to delve into Scripture too deeply before you read about people who suffered from one of the most dreaded skin diseases in history—leprosy. The condition is referred to more than 40 different times in the Bible.

In doing some research on the topic, I found that in my state of Louisiana there was once a major Leprosarium—this is the name they called it a century ago. It was located at the small town of Carville, near the banks of the Mississippi River, about 20 minutes north of Baton Rouge.

Carville had a plantation that was abandoned, and after the Civil War many of the lepers found their way there because it was a place they could be quarantined. In the beginning the facilities were deplorable, but it eventually became state recognized and eventually a federally approved hospital.

This condition is now known as Hansen's Disease

(named after the doctor who isolated the germ that causes leprosy). The hospital was dedicated to the patients as well as finding a cure—which happened in the mid-20th century.

After Hurricane Katrina the sprawling plantation campus that was once home to most of the lepers in the U. S. was converted into a military base.

While reading about the site, and learning there was a small museum dedicated to its history, I decided to take a drive and see for myself.

After passing through the National Guard checkpoint, what I saw was like a snapshot in time, going back 100 years. There, in the amazing museum, was the equipment, photographs, articles, and scientific studies gathered and preserved over the decades.

The hospital building still stands, as well as the living quarters, dining hall, and the cemeteries where the lepers who died were laid to rest. It was an entire self-contained community, with its own farms, dairy cattle, and other livestock.

Still living on the grounds are a few lepers who have been cured of the disease but were already so old that they were unable to integrate back into society.

My interest was piqued, and I spent most of the morning taking pictures, making notes, and gathering information about this fascinating piece of history.

A Startling Truth

As I was about to leave, one of the curators struck up a conversation with me. When she found out that I was a minister and was taking notes that might be used in an upcoming sermon, she asked, "How would you like to meet a man who used to have leprosy?"

"I'd love to," I replied. "If he'd be willing to talk with me."?

"Absolutely," she responded. "He visits occasionally and happens to be here today—and he is my dad!" Then she added, "That's how I came to work here. I was so interested in leprosy that I eventually made it my career."

What a delightful conversation I had with the man who was cured of leprosy around 2004, but had spent about a decade receiving treatment at the hospital.

There were many titbits of wisdom I took away from our meeting, but one statement he made I will never forget. "You know," he began, "leprosy is the inability to feel pain, and because of that we are easily injured on our hands and feet which can quickly turn into infected wounds and before long can spread through our bodies. If they are left unchecked, it leads to debilitation and eventual death."

His statement really captured my attention.

As I began thinking about those words, here was a gentleman who once had the inability to feel pain, but now he was cured. So to him, pain was a gift.

This is certainly a paradigm shift from the way we think about pain—which we all try to avoid at any cost. But in reality, even though it is often unexpected, usually unwanted, and almost always misunderstood, it truly is a gift.

Talk to ten individuals and you will hear ten different stories about pain, whether it is physical, emotional, relational, or caused by some other factor.

Is God Listening?

One of the most dramatic accounts in Scripture took place in the life of a God-fearing righteous man named Job. His journey is foundational and we will follow it in the pages of this book.

We read how *"Satan went out from the presence of the Lord, and struck Job with painful boils from the sole of his foot to the crown of his head. And he took for himself a potsherd with which to scrape himself while he sat in the midst of the ashes"* (Job 2:7-8).

Perhaps the most important fact in these verses is

that Satan had God's permission to strike Job with his ailment. From this truth we can infer that pain does not come from the Almighty, even though at times He may allow it to happen.

You may have prayed for the Lord to take away your pain, yet it continues to plague you. In the natural perhaps you question, "Does God really hear my prayers?" I can unequivocally guarantee that your heavenly Father listens to and hears you, even though He sometimes doesn't answer, or says "Wait," or even "No."

The source of Job's torment was Satan, and the man was suffering spiritual warfare of the highest order. If it were a tornado, it would be ranked an F5!

Please let me explain that I believe there is a huge difference between spiritual warfare and living in a fallen world. Too often, believers blame circumstances on the devil, which he had nothing to do with. After all, there is only one devil and he's not omnipresent. At the moment, he's probably involved in some corner of the world where conflicts are developing, wars are brewing, or disease is mounting.

However, I do know that there are hosts of demons who can inflict pain and suffering on the lives of individuals. While I do not have a scientific study to verify this, it is my opinion that most of our heartaches are not caused by the devil or even demons, but because we live in a fallen world. To put it another way, we live in a fallen climate, on a fallen planet, with sinful people who make bad choices. As a result, we suffer the consequences either in our own lives or in those of our family members because we—or others—have made fallen decisions.

Without question, the Lord uses our circumstances for the transformation of our souls. But I also strongly believe that some of the trials we go through are pure spiritual warfare.

If you are fighting such a battle, you need the help of the Holy Spirit for deliverance. Perhaps there is an addiction, a bondage, or an iniquity that has gained access and grown deep roots in your life. You may need spiritual counseling, or a godly person to lay hands on you and rebuke the enemy.

In the story of Job, God stepped back and permitted Satan to afflict him. Then the devil laughed as Job did his best to push through the pain and suffering.

The Bible does not tell us specifically that Job had leprosy, but that he had a disease of the skin—the largest organ of the body.

At the museum in Carville, when I was talking to the person who had been cured of leprosy and he told me of the damage inflicted on his fingers and toes because they were unable to feel pain, it dramatically altered the way I felt concerning the topic.

God, in His infinite wisdom, designed the human body so that we can feel the sensation of cold and hot, pleasure and pain.

You can tell your toddler a thousand times not to touch the top of the stove because it's hot and will burn him. But just let a youngster put one finger on the stove and he or she will learn more in one second than you can teach in countless warnings. Pain is a great instructor!

ALONG THE BORDER

Since leprosy is a disease that is defined by the inability to feel pain, when Jesus healed the lepers —and He healed dozens—He was in essence restoring their ability to "feel." In other words, He was giving them the *gift* of pain!

I find it interesting that medically, when you're unable to feel pain, it's classified as a disease? That's how important it is to your well being and existence as a human being.

There are many New Testament passages where Jesus healed lepers, but in one account He healed *ten* who had the disease.

As the story unfolds, on His way to Jerusalem, *"Jesus traveled along the border between Samaria and Galilee"* (Luke 17:11 NIV).

If you know a little about New Testament geography, because of the separation of the kingdom of the Old Testament, Israel was still divided into sections. There was Judea situated to the south and Galilee to the north, but in between was a no-man's-land called Samaria.

Jesus traveled frequently in that region. This is where He ministered to the woman at the well, and now we find Him confronting the ten lepers.

Samaritans were considered non-citizens even though they were smack dab in the middle of Israel. The Pharisees and Sadducees (the so-called pure children of Abraham), looked down their noses at them. They were despised and cast out, not even allowed to enter the temple, so they built their own house of worship. Remember, the woman at the well had a discussion with Jesus about "true worship" (John 4:19-24).

The Son of God traveling along the border reminds me of the place where we spend most of our lives—on the border between pain and pleasure. How each of us responds impacts our destiny.

Many individuals wander off course and turn over their lives to seeking pleasure. Others give their days to pain and suffering. In truth, we should pursue neither one, rather seek to become fully devoted followers of Jesus, walking along the border where He is—and in the process learn how to balance ourselves between the two worlds.

A Gift for the Lepers

As Jesus was entering a Samaritan village, *"there met Him ten men who were lepers, who stood afar off"* (Luke 17:12).

They were separated from the residents inside the city walls—outcasts who were not allowed to enter into society.

The book of Leviticus deals very strictly with how to treat victims of leprosy. There was a clear dividing line. If you had the disease, you were to remain outside the city because it was thought you might infect the water or food supply. You were not even allowed to have new clothes or a haircut (Leviticus 13-14).

In Samaria, these ten men stood at a distance, probably at least 20 feet or more away—far enough that they had to shout to attract Jesus' attention.

Scripture tells us, *"And they lifted up their voices and said, 'Jesus, Master, have mercy on us!'"* (Luke 17:13).

They must have known who Jesus was because they called Him by name. Plus, they used the title Rabbi, Teacher, or in this instance it is translated as *Master*.

By saying, *"have pity on us,"* they were not asking for healing, but for a handout. These men wanted food, water, or clothes. In reality, they longed for someone to have compassion and reach out to *touch* them.

One of the Old Testament commands was that if you contracted leprosy you were not allowed to mingle with or be touched by another human being. Can you imagine going through life in such isolation? Surely this is the definition of loneliness.

Jesus must have broken through that 20-foot barrier, because *"when He saw them, He said to them, 'Go, show yourselves to the priests'"* (verse 14).

In Leviticus it is spelled out that if a person was cured from leprosy, they had to walk to the temple and report to the priests. If the religious leaders pronounced them clean they would offer up a special sacrifice which would allow them to reenter society, take up a job, marry, have children, and once again live a normal life.

Jesus, in obeying Leviticus 14, instructed the ten lepers to go and show themselves to the priests.

One of the most powerful lessons of this story is that these men did not receive an instant miracle. The Bible records that *"as they went, they were cleansed"* (Luke 17:14).

Most of the prayers that are answered in our lifetime will not be instantaneous. That's why the word "miracle" is in our vocabulary—because it happens so rarely.

A miracle is what takes place when God suspends the laws of nature such as opening the Red Sea for the children of Israel, causing water to flow out of a rock, or manna to fall from heaven. Seeing blind eyes enjoy the light of day or the lame instantaneously walk still occurs today, but it is rare indeed!

These ten lepers did not receive an instant miracle, instead they were healed in a *process.* And that's the way most of the work God does for us becomes reality.

Please don't get in a hurry. I know the temptation is to cry out, "Make it all go away. I want it to be over."

Sure, you desire for the problem to dissipate, but if you can, just for a moment, stand and listen to the voice of the Spirit. Hear what He is saying to you in your darkest hours. Like the child touching a hot stove, you will learn more in that moment of pain than in a thousand sermons you will hear. The Spirit Himself will be your teacher.

The great British theologian, C. S. Lewis, observed, "God whispers to us in our pleasures, speaks in our consciences, but shouts in our pains."

THE PURPOSE OF YOUR EXISTENCE

What was the reaction when the ten lepers were healed *"as they went"*?

Well, *"one of them, when he saw that he was healed, returned, and with a loud voice glorified God, and fell down on his face at His feet, giving Him thanks"* (Luke 17:15).

I can see him running back, shouting with joy, and throwing himself on the ground in front of Jesus. This was the original Pentecostal worship service!

This individual understood the first duty of humanity. The reason the Creator made you, and the purpose of your existence, is to worship God.

This world will be totally lost and meaningless without a personal understanding of this. Your primary responsibility is to be a worshiper—not just when seated in a pew on Sunday morning, but every day of your life.

Personally, I'm a "front row" worshiper. In the early service at our church, I'm right there from the first down beat of the drum to the last—with both hands lifted up. Even though I can't carry much of a tune, I enjoy singing at the top of my lungs. I don't have much musical talent, but Jesus loves to hear me sing His praises, so I lift my voice to Him.

After all, if I am going to be doing this for eternity, I may as well start practicing now! Yes, I am going to be in His holy presence forever more. I may be on my knees for the first 10,000 years praising His name.

We must never go to heaven a rookie worshiper! When Saint Peter ushers you through the pearly gates, you want to hear him say, "That boy (or girl) is on the front row!"

Let me encourage you to enter into corporate worship, expressing your love for the Lord. Raise you hands, sing aloud, and let Him hear the fruit of praise from your lips. Never be ashamed to open your heart and your voice to God, wherever you sit in the congregation. To me, there is nothing more electrifying than being in a room filled with people who love to worship.

Be like the Samaritan leper who threw himself at Jesus' feet and offered Him praise.

But Jesus asked, *"Were there not ten cleansed? But*

where are the nine? Were there not any found who returned to give glory to God except this foreigner?" (Luke 17:17-18).

Jesus was disappointed in the other nine who were probably children of Abraham, but had forgotten how to worship.

However, there was a special blessing for the solitary one who returned to thank the Lord that the other nine did not receive. Jesus said to him, *"Arise, go your way. Your faith has made you well"* (verse 19).

Some individuals receive their healing or have their prayers answered, but that's where it stops. But to the worshiper who makes the full cycle the supernatural happens. When this *one* came back to Jesus, the Lord recognized his *faith.*

There will never be a day in your life where God will take away faith from the equation —and the more you worship, the greater your trust and expectation. This man was about to have a lifetime of blessings because he worshiped the Lord.

FIVE LIFE-CHANGING TRUTHS

From the story of the ten lepers, there is much we can learn:

First: Life is lived along the border between joy and pain.

Enjoy the journey; not just the good days, but learn to relish the bad ones too. When this happens you know you've crossed the line to maturity.

Second: You are not alone.

You will sometimes feel abandoned and ostracized like the ten lepers, but remember, you are not by yourself. Jesus is on His way.

Third: The answers to your prayers will almost always be a process.

I wish this weren't so, but it is.

From December 2005 to December 2012, I was becoming progressively blind. I earnestly prayed, faithfully stood in healing lines, and fasted—nothing changed.

Then one Sunday morning in the church where I minister, one of our pastors anointed me with oil and prayed for my healing. That day, I knew something supernatural was at work, even though my sight didn't improve.

In fact, after that meeting I failed a driving test and was pronounced legally blind.

I called on Jesus many times, "What's up with this?

Why won't You help me?" He would always reply, "Wait, it's just not your time."

Perhaps you are reading this and are facing a problem that seems insurmountable. You've waited before the Lord, been patient to no avail, and it seems so unfair and unjust. You're tired and want to quit. Let me encourage you to keep holding on.

It took 18 months from the time I felt God touch me, but little by little my sight returned. I woke up one morning and the Lord had almost completely restored my vision.

I don't know why He chooses to move in a process, but in His wisdom, He does. In eternity, this is one of the questions I plan to ask Him.

Fourth: Be thankful even when you don't feel like it.

There is no worship as pure as when it pours out of a broken heart—when you have nothing else to offer other than "I love You, Jesus."

One of the most spectacular worship services I've ever been a part of took place on Sunday morning, September 4, 2005.

On that unforgettable day, I was standing in an empty parking lot with my wife, Rachel, our five children, and about 70 other people. It was six days after Hurricane Katrina roared in from the Gulf of

Mexico and everything we had worked so hard for was gone—our church, our home, our school—all of it was lost, flooded, or damaged beyond repair!

As we gathered on the pavement that morning, our son, Ryan, led the worship service with a box guitar—there was no electricity.

The reason it may have been the purest form of worship I've ever experienced is because we had nothing else to give, other than to tell the Lord, "You alone are the Master of all creation and even though we don't understand Your ways, we trust and believe in You."

Perhaps you are hanging on for dear life at the end of your rope and doubt you have the strength to hold on much longer. Now is the time to dig deep into your soul and be thankful! There is nothing more pleasing to the ears of the Lord than worship that flows from a heart that is broken.

Fifth: Nurture your faith.

This side of eternity, it will be your faith that will pull you through your hardships.

If you are hurting today, listen to the still small voice of the Lord inside you. Remember, God does not initiate your troubles and trials, but He will always use the circumstances of your life to help you become more like Christ.

I'm thrilled you have joined me as we discover more about pain, and how it is an unexpected gift.

Chapter 2

The Purpose of Pain

We've all had first-hand experience with misery and distress. Either we have just come out of a period of pain, are engulfed in one right now, or are about to enter into such a season.

If you share your faith with unbelievers, someone along the way is going to ask, "What is the purpose of all this pain and suffering?"

As a fully devoted follower of Christ, you will need to have an answer to questions like these:

- Why would an all powerful and loving God allow pain and suffering?
- Why are there hungry children in Africa?
- Why do 30-year-old moms die of cancer?
- Why do teenagers get killed in car accidents?
- Why do bad things happen to good people?

I've been wrestling with these question for decades, and pray you will benefit from what I have learned—from the writings of theologians, an in-depth study of God's Word, and divine revelation of the Holy Spirit.

My first experience as a young pastor was in a small church in a small town. Rachel and I were brand new in the ministry and were pastoring a congregation of approximately 70 people at the time. There was a young woman in our church not quite 30 years old. She was married, had two small children, and was a tower of strength in the church. Every time the doors opened, she was on the front row. She was a faithful giver, a volunteer, and a servant to others.

Sadly, this beautiful woman contracted cervical cancer and within three months she died.

I must be honest with you; her passing rocked my world. She was the epitome of faithfulness—a loving wife, a doting mother, a loyal church member, and a fully devoted follower of Christ. I couldn't imagine there being a more perfect example of a believer in our church, yet this horrible disease took her life in a matter of weeks.

I remember presiding over her funeral, standing there with a lump rising in my throat. I was 29, not quite 30 myself, and was really unsure of what words of comfort to say to those who had gathered for the last rites.

Just before I was to deliver my thoughts that morning, those in attendance sang one final song: Amazing Grace. During the hymn, her mother, her sister, and her immediate family seated on the front row quietly stood to their feet, lifted their hands, and worshiped Jesus. It was a spontaneous act of such incredible faith I was blown away. I don't even remember what I said that day, and I'm not even sure if it was intelligible. All I can recall was a family praising and worshiping the Lord in the face of death.

I learned something that day about faith that I would not be able to put in words for years. It was part of the process that has brought me to the views I hold regarding distress and heartache.

Uncovering the Real You

Perhaps you are embroiled in a time of anguish right now—in your health, marriage, finances, or in some other area. If so, you have probably spent time asking God, "Why?"

I have walked in your shoes. I wish that I could tell you that I've never doubted the Lord, never been angry at Him, or questioned His motives. But since I am human, I have.

However, I have learned that God is big enough to take our doubts and fears. If you're angry at Him, He still loves you. If you question your heavenly Father, even if you lose your faith, He still cares for you. In the midst of your trials, He is drawing you ever closer to Himself.

Earlier, I pointed out the fact that God allowed Satan to test Job, which included a time of intense anguish. But when we look at the *purpose* of pain, there is an important aspect of the story we need to understand.

What a predicament. *"Satan went out from the presence of the Lord, and struck Job with painful boils from the sole of his foot to the crown of his head. And he took for himself a potsherd with which to scrape himself while he sat in the midst of the ashes"* (Job 2:7-8).

You would think that at a time like this, Job's wife, for better for worse, would smother him with words of encouragement. But this was not the case. She bluntly said to her husband, *"Do you still hold fast to your integrity? Curse God and die!"* (verse 9).

What about you? Perhaps in your darkest hour you found yourself surrounded by people who were less than supportive.

Even though Job's wife asked in a critical way, "Do you still hold fast to your integrity?" I believe it holds a germ of truth about the purpose of pain.

Maybe it is in the process of our misery that we discover what we're made of. There's a sports axiom that goes like this: football doesn't develop character, it *reveals* it. That statement could be said of basketball, baseball, and every other team sport.

Life doesn't just develop your integrity, it uncovers what's inside. This being the case, pain and suffering actually serve as a way to point out *flaws* in your character. During days of stress you will know yourself better than at any other time. You will discover where your breaking point is and where your vessel leaks.

However, you will need to give an answer to those who question you, and here is Job's reply. He told his wife, *"'You speak as one of the foolish women speaks. Shall we indeed accept good from God, and shall we not accept adversity?' In all this Job did not sin with his lips"* (verse 10).

I doubt this was Job's first rodeo! I think he'd been through trials and tests before and had other episodes of pain and suffering—so he responded from experience.

With you and me, the first couple of times most of us face adversity, we fail miserably. We don't want to accept it; we curse with our lips, doubt the Lord, and in our ordeal, may even deny a higher power. But in the kingdom of God you never really fail a test—you just get scheduled for a retake! Your heavenly Father gives you brand new opportunities to take the exam again.

I don't know about you, but I want to pass His test, and the next one too. I long to learn what God is teaching me.

Ask the Right Question

The problem is that we continually ask the wrong question. We want to know why, why, why, yet God seldom if ever answers "why" questions. Maybe we can't handle the truth, so He protects us.

Instead of asking "Why?" we should be asking "What?"

- "What are you trying to teach me, Lord?"
- "What do I need to learn from this?"
- "What is it that You are developing in me, God?"

If you are in the midst of pain and suffering today, remember the Holy Spirit is your Teacher—ask Him to instruct you so that you may pass through this valley as quickly as possible and reach higher ground.

Will it Happen Here?

Why is it that we accept good from God, yet fail to accept adversity? After all, reverses and rough times are going to be a challenge in the life of every believer, every church, and every generation.

Today, we are appalled and saddened to see the Church of Jesus Christ under enormous persecution. There are militant Muslims beheading Christians in the Middle East, throwing believers overboard from ships, and burning churches across Asia and Africa.

Many in the media may try to make excuses or look the other way, but a modern day Armenian genocide is taking shape right now. And don't be naïve enough to think that the church in the United States will be given a free pass from persecution.

Some of our nation's leading religious observers have come to the conclusion that we are one generation away from Christianity being outlawed in the United States. While we may want to bury our head in the sand and think we are immune, at this very moment legislation is being proposed that will make it a crime for a minister of any church to refuse to perform a gay marriage—or for a church not to underwrite an abortion for an employee.

We need to wake up and remove our blinders!

THE MESSAGE OF THE SHEPHERD

Instead of agonizing when we see the culture and our courts redefining words, laws, and institutions that have stood for hundreds of years, try to see it from another perspective. Could it be that it's about God developing the nature of Christ in us? This is what adversity does. Pain will cause us to wrestle with our integrity. There will be an internal struggle about who we are and what we believe.

Suffering has a way of bringing all these things to the surface. In the midst of your anguish you'll discover and develop your true character.

One of the minor prophets of the Old Testament was Zachariah. He was a shepherd and wrote these words based on his experience: *"So I shepherded the flock marked for slaughter, particularly the oppressed of the flock. Then I took two staffs and called one Favor and the other Union, and I shepherded the flock"* (Zechariah 11:7 NIV).

As you read this verse, keep in mind that if you are a believer, Jesus, the Good Shepherd, is already in your life—and He is there for one reason: to bring favor and union into your Christianity.

If pain does anything, it opens the gate to the Good Shepherd. When Jesus enters into your suffering, you will know Him in a deeper way than ever before:

- You will learn truths about Christ that no pastor can tell you.
- You will experience Him in a way that no song can capture, no author can write, and no conference speaker can teach.
- You will know the Lord in a much more personal way than at any other time in your life.

Sadly, many are so busy trying to alleviate the pain that they don't notice the Shepherd. I pray that you will take a moment to stay silent and listen for the answer as you ask the Lord, "What are you teaching me in this episode of my life?"

THREE PURPOSE-REVEALING TRUTHS

The Apostle Paul wrote extensively about the ravages of pain and suffering. For the cause of Christ, he became the target of agonizing persecution—up until and including the day he was beheaded by

Caesar around 54 A.D.

Paul wrote approximately one third of his New Testament epistles confined to a jail cell as a prisoner. He was pelted with stones, chased out of cities, accused, arrested, and eventually became a martyr for his faith.

What Paul wrote in Colossians unveils the purpose of our suffering and pain:

> *"I now rejoice in my sufferings for you, and fill up in my flesh what is lacking in the afflictions of Christ, for the sake of His body, which is the church, of which I became a minister according to the stewardship from God which was given to me for you, to fulfill the word of God, the mystery which has been hidden from ages and from generations, but now has been revealed to His saints.*
>
> *To them God willed to make known what are the riches of the glory of this mystery among the Gentiles: which is Christ in you, the hope of glory.*
>
> *Him we preach, warning every man and teaching every man in all wisdom, that we may present every man perfect in Christ Jesus.*
>
> *To this end I also labor, striving according to His working which works in me mightily"* (Colossians 1:24-29).

These verses contain three truths regarding the real purpose of our suffering:

First: My pain creates compassion in me for other people.

Notice that Paul states that he rejoiced in his *"sufferings for you"*—in other words, the pain we go through may be for others.

You will develop a depth of compassion for individuals who are in agony with the same problem that tormented you. For example, if you fought a drug addiction you will look with great kindness and mercy on those who are hooked on drugs. If you battled cancer you will feel tremendous empathy for those who are fighting for their lives. If you've been through bankruptcy, divorce, or have buried a loved one, you know better than anyone else the pain they are feeling.

As a result, it gives the Holy Spirit the opportunity to create a love and tenderness in you for others who are suffering. We are to bring love, care, and concern to those who are hurting.

Second: My pain teaches me things that I need to know.

If you remember your days in school, when the

teacher is talking, everyone needs to pay attention and listen. Now, when you are walking the road of heartaches, the Holy Spirit is ready to give you guidance. He is inside you, so as you journey through your pain, be attentive to His voice.

These situations are used by God to build the faith of the believer, but the voice of the Spirit who lives inside of you will give you insight that may not be available from any other source. You will walk out of your season of pain and wonder, "How did I learn that?" It was the input of the Holy Spirit.

Third: My pain empowers me to serve Jesus and His church.

The best advice I can give you is this: turn you misery into ministry!

In the midst of your circumstance, find a man or woman who is worse off than you and begin to serve them. This is the secret to your destiny.

In the above passage, the Apostle Paul speaks of *"the mystery which has been hidden from ages and from generations."* Wow! A mystery is being revealed when you least expect it, in the midst of pain and torment.

The key is found in servanthood, which may seem to be a humble occupation, but there are amazing benefits to the heart and spirit that cannot be measured.

In truth, helping others is one of the highest vocations on the planet. Jesus, the King of Kings said in His mission statement, "I have come to serve!"

At the Last Supper before Christ was arrested and crucified, He asked the disciples, *"For who is greater, he who sits at the table, or he who serves? Is it not he who sits at the table? Yet I am among you as the One who serves"* (Luke 22:27).

Jesus, on His hands and knees, humbly washed the disciples' dusty feet. Why? Because it was a lesson He was trying to instill in us showing an aspect of living we have long forgotten. We are at our greatest when we are humble.

All too often, we find most of the world heaping glory and honor upon themselves, but Jesus said in the Beatitudes, *"Blessed are the meek, for they shall inherit the earth"* (Matthew 5:5).

Who are the meek? The unknown, the unsung hero; the guy who is buried in an unmarked grave, the person who gave his life to care for the orphans, the lepers, the forgotten, or the elderly. It will be these nameless men and women who lived and died not for their own benefit or to gain wealth, power, or fame. Instead, they invested in others; they served!

When Two Worlds Collide

In Bible school, I was pastoring a small church on the weekends, but to help ends meet I took a night job at a funeral home—on the 4:00 PM to 1:00 AM shift. The thing I like about funeral homes is that the customers never complain! And it was usually a very quiet evening.

In the 18 months I worked there we buried the rich and the poor. In fact, I clearly remember when those two worlds collided in one week. The wealthiest man in town passed away on the same day as one of the poorest. They were buried one day apart.

The rich man's funeral was first, and it was an affair attended by every dignitary in the parish. His family purchased the most expensive, gold plated casket.

The following day we arranged a service for a man who came from a family so impoverished that they picked out a cardboard casket; it was all they could afford.

As a young student I was struck by the contrast of these two worlds. I attended both services as we buried both men.

There was one common denominator these two men shared. At the end of the day, they were both dead!

Pain is the great equalizer. It brings the mighty low

and lifts the humble high. It puts us all on a level playing field so that it doesn't matter what your bank account balance is, your address, or the make of the car you drive. Please don't get me wrong. We should all strive to do the best we can, but earthly riches must never be our objective. It's not worth losing your way in this world, forsaking God and trying to accumulate "things."

Let your life be measured by the service you give to Jesus and His church. God loves the rich and the poor equally; He created us all in His image. Whatever category you are in, there's no virtue in poverty, but neither is it found in wealth. There is virtue only in the blood of Jesus Christ.

May we all be able to echo the words of Paul, *"That I may know Him and the power of His resurrection, and the fellowship of His sufferings, being conformed to His death"* (Philippians 3:10).

Following Jesus will challenge and change you, helping you to dream bigger dreams and accomplish greater things for His kingdom. He will take you places you never thought you would go and raise the sights of your life with the power of His resurrection.

However, we must never forget that the coin has two sides. There's quite a contrast between *"the power of His resurrection"* and *"the fellowship of His sufferings."*

The word "fellowship" in this verse is *koinonia,* Greek for brotherhood. We are counseled to always love the biological brothers and sisters we were raised with—for no one else knows the chapters of your life like they do. Why? Because they've walked beside you and lived your story. That's why you will be forever connected to them. It's *koinonia,* the shared experience.

This is a factor that plays out on a grander scale in the church. As believers, we all have a shared story: that we were trapped in sin until we met the living Christ. We found forgiveness, were born again, filled with His Spirit, delivered from the darkness of our pain and suffering, and set on a new path. This is the *koinonia* we share.

THE MIGHTY, THE MEEK, AND THE MASTER

In the opening scene of *Lord Of The Rings,* when the brotherhood of the ring is formed, it is an epic picture of a group of misfits and mighty coming together. And the weakest of them all —*the hobbits*— are chosen to bear the ring—which would give them power over others. They all put their lives on the line for the sake of the call.

No one is seeking his own glory, power, or fame.

They all have one reason and one reason alone to exist, and that is to destroy evil and set the people of Middle Earth free.

To me, this is an allegory of today's church; that the mighty and the meek are united together in this unique brotherhood of the shared story. We lay aside our own fame and glory and work together for the common good—for the freedom of those that we haven't even met. And usually, the most unlikely of us all bears the ring.

It's really about you. Yes, you are the bearer of the ring. You are the sharer of the story, and you'll either be a victim or a victor, a chump or a champion. Will you be crushed in the ashes or rise as the Phoenix?

Here's what it all boils down to: what will you do with Christ? That is exactly why He was chosen to bear the cross—and in His pain He redeemed us all. That is the fellowship that we join; the fellowship of His suffering.

As part of the Greatest Story Ever Told, the purpose of your pain is to help you become more like Jesus.

Chapter 3

The Process of Pain

Whether we like it or not, we are all going through a process.

The one thing I've learned about my heavenly Father is that He not only *thinks* He is God—He is! God with a capital G!

Sometimes we forget that His plans are different than ours and His schedule is not like our schedule, but we work on His timetable.

The journey the Lord has implemented on earth is a divinely ordered progression. Sometimes it is painful for us to endure, but there is a reason behind every path He places before us. Since His ways and thoughts are higher than ours, it only makes sense to go ahead and acquiesce to His agenda.

As we continue to examine the life of Job, it seems like everything that *could* go wrong *did!* There was one calamity after another and he found himself in a terrible situation that grew from bad to worse.

Not only did he have to endure sores covering his

entire body, but his wife renounced God and lost her faith. His children were killed by a windstorm. All of his livestock were either destroyed or stolen and Job was left destitute.

As Scripture records:

> *Now there was a day when his sons and daughters were eating and drinking wine in their oldest brother's house; and a messenger came to Job and said, "The oxen were plowing and the donkeys feeding beside them, when the Sabeans raided them and took them away—indeed they have killed the servants with the edge of the sword; and I alone have escaped to tell you!"*
>
> *While he was still speaking, another also came and said, "The fire of God fell from heaven and burned up the sheep and the servants, and consumed them; and I alone have escaped to tell you!"*
>
> *While he was still speaking, another also came and said, "The Chaldeans formed three bands, raided the camels and took them away, yes, and killed the servants with the edge of the sword; and I alone have escaped to tell you!"*
>
> *While he was still speaking, another also*

came and said, "Your sons and daughters were eating and drinking wine in their oldest brother's house, and suddenly a great wind came from across the wilderness and struck the four corners of the house, and it fell on the young people, and they are dead; and I alone have escaped to tell you!" (Job 1:13-19).

The truth we can glean from this passage is that often, our pain and suffering will appear to be more than we think we can bear.

You see other people in dire circumstances and may either be moved or unmoved by their plight, but when it is *yours,* it has all of your attention. You may even cry out, "This is the worst thing that has ever happened to me"—and from your perspective it may be. You're dealing with it 24 hours a day. You go to bed hurting, then wake up and the pain is still there.

However, what you are feeling is *your* point of view, not God's. Let me assure you that your heavenly Father always changes the equation. When the Lord adds His grace to any situation, it alters the outcome.

When you and I are struggling through heartaches in our own strength, we can barely make it. But when we factor in the grace and mercy of God, we have the ability to overcome. So when you pray concerning your pain, ask the Lord to remove it if possible, but don't let your prayer end there.

Get down on your knees and tell God, "If You choose not to remove this suffering (which He has every right to do) then please give me the grace to walk through this valley."

A Gift Called "Weakness"

Paul the Apostle was tested much like Job. It wasn't God who brought trouble upon him, but the devil. As Paul writes, *"Lest I should be exalted above measure by the abundance of the revelations, a thorn in the flesh was given to me, a messenger of Satan to buffet me"* (2 Corinthians 12:7).

Then the apostle states, *"Concerning this thing I pleaded with the Lord three times that it might depart from me. And He said to me, 'My grace is sufficient for you, for My strength is made perfect in weakness'"* (verses 8-9).

When you think your burden is too much to carry, grace will enter the picture and make the difference. You will be astounded by what you discover hidden inside the amazing grace of God. The meaning of your pain will be revealed to you in the hour of your greatest need, because when grace meets your suffering, you have a new, fresh perspective.

This is why Paul could declare, *"Therefore I take pleasure in infirmities, in reproaches, in needs, in persecutions, in distresses, for Christ's sake. For when I am weak, then I am strong"* (verse 10).

In other words, his weakness was a gift from Almighty God.

OTHERS SUFFER TOO

So often, when we are processing our pain, we expect more compassion and sympathy from the people around us than they are able to deliver. I've been guilty of this, and perhaps you have too. When I am going through a hard time, I expect that my wife, my best friend, or my brother should be able to identify with me, but often they can't.

While others may be able to sit with you, hold your hand, pray out loud, and cry with you, it's doubtful they will have the ability to fix what's broken on the inside.

In Job's distress, those who knew and loved him gathered around him. The Bible tells us:

> *Now when Job's three friends heard of all this adversity that had come upon him, each*

one came from his own place—Eliphaz the Temanite, Bildad the Shuhite, and Zophar the Naamathite. For they had made an appointment together to come and mourn with him, and to comfort him.

And when they raised their eyes from afar, and did not recognize him, they lifted their voices and wept; and each one tore his robe and sprinkled dust on his head toward heaven.

So they sat down with him on the ground seven days and seven nights, and no one spoke a word to him, for they saw that his grief was very great (Job 2:11-13).

These men didn't casually drop by and sit with Job for an hour or two, but stayed an entire week! As his friends, they recognized that his pain and sorrow was so grave that no one uttered a word. They were overcome by his grief and sat in stunned silence.

Job was probably hoping that these three friends were bringing an answer. Maybe they were going to loan him some money, buy him some cattle, talk sense into his wife, or maybe just cover his sores with a soothing balm or oil, but they did nothing! They just sat there and commiserated with his pain, cried, stared, and waited in awkward silence.

Please understand that, at times, those around you may seem unwilling or unable to help you, but we must not make the mistake of blaming them. They are most likely suffering too.

THE PARALYSIS OF FEAR

These three men had walked a long distance, taken valuable time off work, left their families, and spent their own money to be by his side. I'm sure they each had their own problems and were not capable of meeting all of Job's needs. Yet they were joining him in the spirit of friendship, recognizing his pain.

Have you found yourself in the same place as Job—hurting, abandoned, and lonely? You're crying out for help and those you thought would lend a hand aren't measuring up. Be careful not to become bitter. The enemy would like nothing more than for your pain to turn into animosity. If that happens it will further separate you from sincere relationships.

It may not come as a surprise, but Job began to take his suffering out on his friends. He grows angry and starts blaming them, forgetting that they are hurting too. Let me remind you that every man or woman you come in contact with this week is suffering in some form or another. Your next door neighbor, the person in front of you at the checkout counter, the driver in the car next to you.

Then Job began cursing the day he was ever born. *"Why did I not die at birth? Why did I not perish when I came from the womb?"* (Job 3:11).

He wished he was dead, or at least had the courage to kill himself. Then he began to speak curses over his life.

To some extent, we all do this. When things get so out control, we may think:

- "Why did I ever try?"
- "Why did I marry this person?"
- "Why did I buy that house, or car?"
- "Why did I start that business?"

Wallowing in his grief, Job cried out, *"For the thing I greatly feared has come upon me, and what I dreaded has happened to me"* (verse 25).

As fully devoted followers of Jesus Christ, we have chosen a life of faith, but all too often we revert back to our old nature and, even though we are saved, we become people of fear.

When the torment began, Job worried that he would lose everything—and his worst nightmare came true.

Don't Look Back!

Regardless of how terrible the circumstances may be, let me challenge you to reverse the pattern in your life—instead of being a man or woman of fear, put your trust in the Lord and become a person of faith. Instead of anticipating the worst, expect the best.

I will give you an example. Let's say your spouse is an hour late coming home from work and your mind goes into overdrive. You immediately assume he or she is in a car accident. Instead of contemplating the worst, why not assume something wonderful, like maybe they stopped by a restaurant to bring home a gourmet meal!

Poor Job. In his self-pity he complained, *"I am not at ease, nor am I quiet; I have no rest, for trouble comes"* (verse 26).

We have a word in the English language to express the lack of ease, it's called *disease.* If you are physically ill, we say your body has a disease; if you're emotionally distraught we say you have an emotional disease.

Perhaps you have lost all your peace and tranquility and you have no place of quiet to rest. Please don't panic. This is common to *all* of us—big and small, young and old, rich and poor. It's another equalizer of mankind.

Job also made the mistake of looking back too long. Occasionally it is necessary to look in the rearview mirror when we're driving, but not more than a moment.

The same is true about life. You can glance back and reflect to see how far you've come, but if you take your eyes off where you're headed for very long, you will wind up in a ditch!

One of the truths we can take from Job is that we will be tempted to relive the past and regret the decisions that brought us to where we are now. This is a trap. While you should take account of what has happened and accept responsibility for what you decided upon, you can't make it a campsite and stay there indefinitely, or you'll become a prisoner to your past.

The enemy of your soul would like nothing more than to rob your tomorrow by trapping you in your yesterday. Sure, there are decisions you have made, but there are no do-overs. This is why the Apostle Paul wrote: *"Forgetting those things which are behind and reaching forward to those things which are ahead, I press toward the goal for the prize of the upward call of God in Christ Jesus"* (Philippians 3:13-14).

THE GREAT EXCHANGE

When you accept Christ as your Savior, all He asks is that you acknowledge your sins, own your bad decisions, and then repent of them. He doesn't make you relive every bad choice or sin that you have committed. It's as simple as this: *"If you confess with your mouth the Lord Jesus and believe in your heart that God has raised Him from the dead, you will be saved"* (Romans 10:9).

God asks that we take responsibility for our trespasses, then we turn everything over to Christ. It's the great exchange: we trade our old to Him for His new. We give Him our sins and He gives us His righteousness; we present Him our bad, and He transforms it into good.

So if God, in His mercy, will give the priceless gift of eternal life on that principle, how much more will He do for the situation in which you find yourself today?

THREE PRINCIPLES TO REMEMBER

Concerning the process of pain, here's what we have learned:

First: Your pain and suffering will appear to be more than you think you can tolerate. This is just an appearance, so don't be tricked. It may look as if it's too big a problem for God to handle, but nothing is impossible with Him.

Second: The people around you may seem to be unwilling or unable to help you, but never turn the tables and blame them. Remember, they are suffering too.

Third: You will be tempted to relive the past and to regret the decisions that brought you to where you are. This is a trap you must avoid.

A Profound Statement

You may wonder, "Where do I go to process my pain?"

I heard this asked in a conversation with a friend 25 years ago. I was a young Bible college student just starting my ministry and I had internalized a lot of issues. We can process our distress one of two ways: we can either thrust it on everyone around us through bitter or angry words, or try to bury it deep down within ourselves. I was an *internalizer*—and I discovered that one is just as bad as the other.

When I was hurt or offended I would immediately

bury my feelings. Of course, when you're young you can do that for a while, but eventually it fills up your soul and begins to eat away at your heart. There will come a breaking point where you can't cover it up any longer and it will explode, either through your health, emotions, or relationships.

I was at that point when my friend made a comment in passing that has stuck with me all these years. He told me, "Process your pain at the cross."

I don't think he had any idea how profoundly his statement impacted me. It was as if he wasn't even talking, but it was the voice of Jesus that I was hearing. Those words leapt into my soul and a light flashed on in my mind. For the first time I saw the place I was supposed to be bringing my pain.

If you are hurting and you've tried telling others about it, or you've attempted to bury it, let me recommend this third option: process your pain at the cross.

In the words of the prophet Isaiah, *"Surely He has borne our griefs and carried our sorrows; yet we esteemed Him stricken, smitten by God, and afflicted. But He was wounded for our transgressions, He was bruised for our iniquities; the chastisement for our peace was upon Him, and by His stripes we are healed"* (Isaiah 53:4-5).

That took place at Calvary, in Jerusalem 2000 years ago.

It's All Covered

There are six pains listed in the above passage and they cover every aspect of human suffering—psychological, spiritual, emotional, physical and relational. Every area of human anguish and despair is bound up in these two verses. Each of them was put on Christ—(1) your griefs, (2) your sorrows, (3) your transgressions, (4) your iniquities, (5) your chastisement, (6) your stripes.

We all have issues we are grieving over, people or possessions we have lost, or blessings we have missed out on. It's a grieving process, but Jesus bore it all.

There are events or actions for which we are sorrowful. But I am delighted to tell you that Christ covered them too.

Transgressions are sins including the acts of omission or commission we have committed against God, other people, or ourselves. Jesus took them upon Himself.

Our iniquities—a bondage or a deep held addiction. It is that thing you secretly run to for comfort when life isn't going well. Those are hidden sins, yet Jesus bore them at Calvary.

Chastisement is the beating that we take in this world, physically and relationally. Jesus also suffered this for us.

By His stripes we are made whole. He paid for our healing—every disease, every disorder, every emotional trauma, every distress. All you've been afflicted with in life was put on Christ at the cross.

Too often Christians try to carry the weight of their own problems, but God didn't call you to be a beast of burden like an ox; He called you to be the sheep of His pasture—and sheep are not burden-bearers.

Jesus is telling each of us today, *"Come to Me, all you who labor and are heavy laden, and I will give you rest. Take My yoke upon you and learn from Me, for I am gentle and lowly in heart, and you will find rest for your souls. For My yoke is easy and My burden is light"* (Matthew 11:28-30).

Before Christ's arrest and crucifixion, He told the apostle John that He would be returning to heaven, *"And I will pray the Father, and he shall give you another Comforter, that he may abide with you for ever; even the Spirit of truth; whom the world cannot receive, because it seeth him not, neither knoweth him: but ye know him; for he dwelleth with you, and shall be in you. I will not leave you comfortless: I will come to you"* (John 14:16-18 KJV).

In the Greek, the word "Comforter" is *Paraclete*,

one who comes along side and carries our burden. We are not supposed to be weighted down with problems. This is why we collapse and fall into sin. We make bad choices because we are lugging a load of sorrow we were never designed to shoulder.

Remember, Christ is your Good Shepherd, and He will carry you when you can't carry on!

Symbols of the cross have been reconstructed all over our planet. We see them displayed across our nation as we travel. Why? Because the cross is the hope of the world. You can bring your addictions, sin, sorrows, grief, embarrassment, and your worst moments to the cross and Christ will not judge you. He will only offer His forgiveness and love.

There's a sanctuary called "Oude Kirk" (Old Church) sitting near the harbor in Amsterdam, Holland. It's been there since the year 1306. In 1620, a group of Pilgrims left that spot and sailed to Plymouth, England, and eventually to America on the *Mayflower.*

Today, erected on that church is an amazing cross that stands as a constant reminder of the Hope of the World.

What an awesome gift God gave!

Chapter 4

The Pain of Poverty

As citizens of the most blessed nation on the earth, it is easy to forget that most of the world lives in abject poverty. In fact, eighty percent of its inhabitants exist on just two or three dollars a day.

Before I became a lead pastor, I was a missions pastor for years and led teams around the globe. So I've witnessed poverty first hand. I have walked through the slums of Mexico where a million people live in cardboard huts near garbage dumps. I've been across Africa, where countless die due to lack of clean water or food, and we have sent missions teams to Haiti, one of the poorest nations of all.

Let me share one thing I have learned: poverty was never meant to be a place where people permanently live—it's a stop on a journey to becoming what God wants us to be.

I have also come to the conclusion that in an abundant land like America, men and women rarely live in poverty unless it's a choice. There are too many jobs that people refuse to take.

However, there are millions living in dire circumstances—not just financially, but in their marriage, health, or relationships.

Last spring, while thinking about this topic, I decided to plant a garden on an acre of land we own. Rachel and I thought it would be an adventure to try our hand at being farmers, and it became a baptism by dirt! I never had so much soil under my fingernails in my life.

Soon I found myself up every morning at 5:30, pulling on my rubber boots and going out into the garden. Between us we didn't have much knowledge, but Rachel's dad knows a lot about farming and had been teaching us the ropes.

In one area we planted four rows of corn seeds, and it is truly amazing what happens when the soil, the water, and the temperature all play their part. About 14 days later, small seedlings began to pop out of the ground.

What's Inside?

One Sunday, I decided to use my experience to teach some principles from God's Word.

I took the corn seeds that were left over, put six or eight seeds in little packets and had the ushers hand them out to those in attendance.

I was so proud of what was happening, I showed a picture on a big screen of the corn actually pushing through the ground to reach the sun. At the time, the stalks were about a foot tall.

The real seed is not what you see with your eyes, it's what's inside. The exterior is just a shell, or a husk; the life is in the embryo tucked inside.

This replicates you and me. Our bodies are shells, seed holders. But inside each of us is the embryo of life, our spirit.

When God plants you, perhaps you feel hidden away, forgotten, and that the Lord has put you in a situation of impossibilities. If you ever reach the place where you throw up your hands in despair and say, "I don't know what to do next," wait on God. Trust that He is able to see you through, knowing that He has a plan that is far greater than anything you can imagine.

The reason that most people fail to see their potential and destiny is because they are not patient, put the cart before the horse, and don't allow God to take His time with them. They want it *their* way.

Maybe you feel buried today and can't understand what is happening around you. Just like the tiny embryo inside the shell of the corn seed, in the midst of our pain, God hides us from the world, and covers us deep in His love.

Most individuals never see the harvest of their seed because, impatiently, they dig their way out of the ground far too early, thus defeating the purposes of God.

Is There a Lack of Resources?

Around our globe, out of seven billion people, six billion live in near-destitution. It's not because there is a lack, but the pain of poverty is a product of fallen man and the present condition of his wicked heart.

For example, Haiti is one of the poorest nations, but there is enough gold buried in the earth beneath the island of Hispaniola to make every Haitian on the island rich. However, most of the gold is being exploited by the government and by other powers around the world. What's the result? The poor remain poor.

Alaska has an abundance of oil, but there the situation is entirely different. If you are a resident and have lived in the state for a full calendar year, you receive an annual dividend check from the oil that comes out of the reserve. The check for 2015 was $2,072.

Can you imagine if Haiti did the same thing? If they designated the proper use for all the gold they extract, poverty would be eliminated in one day.

After the devastating earthquake of January 2010, the world raised more than $1 billion dollars for Haiti. These generous donations barely changed a thing because most of the funds were exploited by government corruption and thievery. Sadly, It never really reached the poor.

Think of our own nation. In the past 50 years we have spent $20 *trillion* in the war on poverty—yet there are more poor people in the U. S. than ever before.

I hope you see the parallel. It's not because of a lack of resources; it is because of the mismanagement of seed.

Satan's First Attack

Today, I pray you will realize that God has not only gifted you with seed, but has given you the responsibility of what to do with it. There are enough natural resources in our world at this very moment for every family on the planet to live in comfort. To be specific, there are about 2.5 billion family units on the earth today and there's enough food, water, and wealth that they could all live in comfort. So what happens? Why do most people live their lives in poverty? Why can they never escape the systems of darkness?

God never intended for His creation to scrape by, scratching out a living. It was a result of the fall of man and now it's enforced by the wickedness of the human heart. But in the Lord's view, life is a journey that we take to the land of plenty, but most people never find their way.

As we look back to the story of Job, we can see the problem from his angle. We are told, *"Now there was a day when his sons and daughters were eating and drinking wine in their oldest brother's house; and a messenger came to Job and said, 'The oxen were plowing and the donkeys were feeding beside them, when the Sabeans raided them and took them away—indeed, they have killed the servants with the edge of the sword; and I alone have escaped to tell you'"* (Job 1:13-15).

The first attack launched by the devil on Job was on the seeds of his field. When the Lord gave Satan permission to afflict God's servant, the evil one went to the place he was sowing, stole the animals that were plowing, killed the workers he had hired, and destroyed the seeds in the ground.

Three Timeless Truths

There are basic principles we need to learn concerning Satan, soil, and seeds.

Truth #1: The first thing the enemy of your soul will attack will be your seeds.

My father-in-law taught me, "If you are going to sow an acre of corn it will take a 50 pound bag of grain containing 30 to 40 thousand seeds. Then, when harvest time comes, it will reap 35 thousands ears of corn." That's astounding!

So how can you go from one bag that would fit on your shoulder to three months later reaping so many ears of corn that it would take a locomotive train car to move them all? It is because of the law of the seed.

This is why the enemy knows where to strike first—in your finances, your family, your business, and your emotional health.

The farmer knows this, so when the harvest is ready, first thing he sets aside is his "seed corn." The first ten percent is taken, brought to a barn, and not touched because this is what he uses to sow the next season's harvest.

The reason most people live in lack is because they

eat their seed. When you receive your income from your job or investments, the first seed belongs to Jesus. You take it and you put it in the barn, in this case into His house, because it is the seed for your future reaping.

Many live paycheck to paycheck, in debt up to their eyeballs, barely surviving, because they continually devour their seed.

You may think, "Well, my "ten percent" seeds are only $100 a week, or $1,000 a month—or whatever your income may be. We must never underestimate the potential of one small packet of seeds.

In 1981, when Rachel and I were married, I was making a $150.76 a week. We tithed on that income to the penny. I would give God $15.08. It took a great deal of faith because we were barely making ends meet. But we were faithful.

Some may say, "Well, $15 isn't that much. Why didn't you just keep it?"

I knew it wasn't mine, it was God's, and I was planting seeds.

At the time I was in Bible college, we didn't own a house and had an old run-down car. But let me tell you this: I never won the lottery; I didn't have a rich benefactor who died and left me a million dollars in his will. But because I planted seeds along the way,

I've reaped a harvest that has become greater and greater.

As a minister, I hear this again and again from those who don't tithe. These are the ones who complain, "We're struggling," or "We are going under."

They seem surprised, yet they have eaten their seed. If your marriage is in trouble, it may be because you're not planting seeds in your spouse. You are not sowing love, kindness, gentleness, and servant-heartedness. Whatever you receive out of your marriage is directly related to what you invest into the union.

We must raise our children the same way. Sow into them what you want them to reap in the generation to follow, into your grandchildren.

Job's friend Eliphaz told him, *"But as for me, I would seek God, and to God I would commit my cause—who does great things, and unsearchable, marvelous things without number. He gives rain on the earth, and sends water on the fields"* (Job 5:8-10).

The conversation was about planting a harvest.

When the enemy determines to destroy you, he will always attack your seeds, your fields, your harvest. But never forget that it is God who brings the rain that will water your crop!

Truth #2: The Lord is your source, but you are the farmer.

What are you doing with your God-given seeds?

When Jesus died for us, His body was buried in the earth because it was going to produce a harvest. As believers, when you pass from this life, your physical remains are placed in the ground, but it is only so your spirit can be freed to live forever; it's eternal. This principal works in your life, in your health, in your finances, and in your ministry.

During Christ's last week on earth, before He would be arrested, tried, crucified, and buried, He came into Jerusalem riding on a young donkey. The people took branches of palm trees and ran out to meet Him. It was during the feast of Passover.

There were more than a hundred thousand Jews and Hebrews in Jerusalem that day who came from every known nation. In addition, the Bible tells us, *"Now there were certain Greeks among those who came up to worship at the feast. Then they came to Phillip, who was from Bethsaida of Galilee"* (John 12:20-21).

Bethsaida was a Greek speaking area in Israel that Philip, one of the 12 disciples, called home. These visitors from Greece probably heard Philip talking and thought he was someone they could relate to—since he spoke their language and was one of Jesus' staff members. So they went to him and said, *"Sir, we wish to see Jesus"* (verse 21).

This is the request that should be in the heart of every human being on the planet.

Phillip now had a quandary. There were people all around wanting to see the Lord. So, *"Philip came and told Andrew [another disciple], and in turn Andrew and Philip told Jesus"* (verse 22).

Andrew likely said, "I know there's a huge demand on Your time. People want to talk to You and have You pray for them. But there is a group of Greeks over here who really want to see You."

Notice how Jesus responded to this request. As He did so often, He did not give them a direct answer, but replied with a question or a statement. On this occasion, Jesus said, *"The hour has come that the Son of Man should be glorified"* (verse 23)—and then began talking about *seeds.*

When Philip and Andrew heard this they must have thought, "What? What does that even mean? These Greeks want to talk to You and You're saying that Your hour has come?"

The reason Jesus spoke this way is because He always reads the motives of people's hearts.

You have probably experienced this when an

individual broaches the subject of an offense, complaint, or trouble. They hardly ever tell you what's really going on. Instead, they will just circle the outskirts or the perimeter of the issue.

Jesus would just ignore all the clutter and hit right to the heart of the matter.

By saying that the "Son of Man should be glorified," the Lord wanted them to recognize their source. Then came a powerful principle.

Truth #3: Your increase is in your seed.

This is how the story is told in the Message translation. Jesus began, *"Listen carefully"* (John 12:24). He was letting all those within the sound of His voice know that what He was about to tell them was important.

Jesus continued, *"Unless a grain of wheat is buried in the ground, dead to the world, it is never any more than a grain of wheat"* (verse 24 MSG).

The three greatest crops on the earth today are corn, rice, and potatoes. Wheat is in the top ten. This being true, there is enough wheat, corn, rice, soybeans, and a few other crops this year to feed every human being in our world.

- There is no lack of food, there's a shortage of people planting seeds.
- There is no lack of water, there's a shortage of people digging wells.

My friend Bishop Holmes digs wells in Uganda. There's enough for every village to have a source of running water, but there is a lack of wells.

In our lives, there are plenty of resources at our disposal, but they are wasted by lack of faith and a lack of work.

Jesus is explaining that unless a seed is planted in the ground, it remains nothing more than grain. Useless —chicken feed at best!

"But if it is buried"—well, there lies a different story.

You see, when God buries us, He takes over, and that's not a bad place to be. He covers us in His love and gives us the opportunity to grow.

Every seed planted in the ground gets in harmony with its environment, and with the right balance of water and sun, it pushes through the soil and shoots up. This is the law of creation that applies to every part of our lives.

Jesus said, *"But if it is buried, it sprouts and reproduces itself many times over"* (verse 24 MSG).

It's impossible to estimate how many apple trees can be reproduced from one apple, or how many stalks of corn are in one seed, because each generation will produce new seeds to plant. This is why, being a good steward of God's resources, you protect every seed, no matter how small.

Jesus continued to drive home this point: *"In the same way, anyone who holds on to life just as it is destroys that life"* (verse 25 MSG).

A truth many ignore or are reluctant to face is that none of us are going to escape this earth alive. The Bible says, *"It is appointed for men to die once..."* (Hebrews 9:27).

Unless Jesus returns during our lifetime, we will all go by way of the grave.

Millions are attempting to hold on to life "just the way it is." They waste their days on the desires of the flesh, on the lust of their own bodies, or on what the mind thinks it needs.

This is a trap of the enemy. The more we get, the more we need, and the more we hoard, the more we keep—and the more miserable we become along the way. Why? Because, as followers of Christ we weren't called to be hoarders, we were called to be planters and sowers.

Time to Get Reckless!

Each man or woman is allotted a certain number of years on this earth. This is why Jesus told us that anyone who holds on to life just as it is destroys that life. Then He added, *"But if you let it go, reckless in your love, you'll have it forever, real and eternal"* (John 12:25 MSG).

If you want to know the key to a happy marriage, try being *recklessly* in love with your spouse! Men, every morning, wake up and say, "Girl, every day, more and more, I'm crazy in love with you!"

She may think you need a cup of coffee, or your having a dream, but just be recklessly in love!

- Want to know how to have a successful business? Do reckless things. Serve above and beyond what your customers would ever expect.
- Want to be financially secure? Be reckless and give to God more than He asks.
- Want to be a productive farmer? Be reckless and plant more seeds than you can ever harvest. Give away the surplus.

Since you only get one life, why are you holding

back? What are you waiting for?

Remember, Jesus promised that if you let it go and are reckless in your love, *"you'll have it forever, real and eternal."*

What you see with your eyes is only the outer shell of the seed. One day it will die, and the real life will spring up and last without end. This is why I am warning you as strongly as I can, not to eat your seed. Plant it! Give it! Serve it! Water it! Love it! Be reckless with it!

Jesus said, *"If any of you wants to serve me, then follow me. Then you'll be where I am, ready to serve at a moment's notice. The Father will honor and reward anyone who serves me"* (verse 25 MSG).

The Lord finally got around to answering Phillip and Andrew: "Oh, they want to see Me? They want to talk to Me? Tell them to follow Me; then they'll be where I am—ready to serve at a moment's notice."

Most never reap a harvest because they are too busy or too lazy to plant the seed. They aren't served because they fail to serve others. They desire the Father's honor and reward, yet don't want to die to receive His gift.

Are we willing to die to self, to this world, to our sin? Only then are the blessings and favor of God released into our lives.

May you mirror a seed, breaking out of the ground and lifting your hands toward heaven. There is no telling what wonders the Lord will produce in you.

Practical, Positive Steps

When you understand that your increase is contained in you seed, everything changes.

If you truly want to escape poverty, here are some practical, positive steps:

- Be a good steward of your financial seeds.
- Calculate your debt and determine your net worth.
- Plan for your retirement.
- Live on a budget.

Much of the pain of poverty is self inflicted. If it is your genuine desire to serve God and prepare for an abundant future, try the 10-10-80 plan. For every dollar you receive, tithe 10%, save or invest 10%, live on 80%. It's that simple.

The Creator did not place you on this earth to deteriorate or decay. You were planted as a divine seed to burst forth, flourish, increase, and multiply for His kingdom.

Chapter 5

The Pain of Betrayal

Have you ever shared a secret in confidence, only to have a friend treat it as gossip? Has someone you totally trusted lied to your face?

You're not alone. It's common to humanity that we have felt the sting of betrayal.

As we look at pain from many points of view, it parallels the truths found in the book of Job.

The phrase "Job's comforters" has come into our popular language to describe individuals who mean to help, but seem much more concerned with their own feelings and needs than they are with the other person. So they end up throwing coals on the fire and making things worse!

We are introduced to Job's three so-called comforters—Eliphaz, Bildad, and Zophar—starting in Job 4. At first they were silent, but then they began to talk.

Catch the sarcasm in Job's words when he answers his friends, saying, *"Doubtless you are the only people who matter, and wisdom will die with you!"* (Job 12:2 NIV).

Let's face it, we're not exactly thrilled when people talk down to us—when they treat us like they are superior. Then Job goes into a self-defense mode: *"But I have a mind as well as you; I am not inferior to you. Who does not know all these things?"* (verse 3 NIV).

Job was basically telling them, "You guys are full of yourselves and I am just as smart as you."

I fully understand the human need to self-protect and to defend our integrity, but I'm not sure that it's always necessary. I've been guilty of it a thousand times, but question whether it does any good. It may make us feel better to vent and tell people off, stating our own case, but in the end it rarely accomplishes the intended objective.

Next, Job begins to call his comforters out, which I believe is necessary for honest, real relationships. He said, *"I am one mocked by his friends"* (verse 4).

Job's three friends came to his aid, but they did everything but rescue him. This is why he chastised them, "Let me tell you what you've done. You have mocked me and betrayed me." Then he declared, *"[I] called on God and He answered"* (verse 4). And he added, "I am *'just and blameless'* yet you ridicule me."

In the midst of your pain and suffering, it's good to hold onto a reasonable understanding of your identity. If you will pay attention, you will discover a tremendous amount about yourself during a time of chaos.

As we have mentioned, during his ordeal, Job lost everything he held dear—his wealth, his wife, his children, his home, his farm, and his health. In a matter of a few days, he went from a wealthy married man with sons, daughters, and much land and cattle, to a person who was destitute. His body was tormented with sores from head to toe and he was laying in the dust of what was once his former ranch.

Yet there was one thing Job did not lose—his identity.

When his three friends arrived on the scene, he probably thought, "They're coming to help. Here come's the cavalry! They want to rescue me from my troubles."

Instead, however, they mocked him, blamed him, and belittled him. The people he most trusted became a huge disappointment.

Was it God's Punishment?

In order to have the full picture of what Job faced, let me encourage you to read the entire story in the Old Testament.

Job's first friend was Eliphaz, who told him, "Hey Job, God is punishing you for your sins." As it is recorded in Job 4:7-9: *"Remember now, who ever perished being innocent? Or where were the upright ever cut off? Even as I have seen, Those who plow iniquity and sow trouble reap the same. By the blast of God they perish, and by the breath of His anger they are consumed."*

Please understand, when you are down and out and your friends are telling you that this is a judgment from God, that's bad counsel. They are unfamiliar with the nature and character of God. The Almighty is not punitive. If we all received our just dues, we would be struck by lightning about every ten seconds!

It's just the opposite:

- God is a God of love.
- He's a God of mercy.
- He's a defender.
- He's a protector.
- He's a helper.
- He's a friend.
- He's a rescuer.
- He is a forgiver.

Eliphaz, however, had a very weak understanding

of who God truly is. That's why he told Job, "God is punishing you!"

I have noticed that betrayers may attack out of a spiritual motive, but in reality, they have a shallow awareness of God. What may be couched in religious terms or even the use of Scripture to defend their opinion can sometimes be off-base. If they really knew the Lord, they would not betray you as they have.

Friend, God does not punish people for their sins, instead He sent His Son to take all of your punishment on Himself. According to Isaiah 53:3, Jesus was *"A Man of sorrows"*—not because He was a sorrowful Man, but because He took your sin, your disease, your iniquities, all of your suffering, and He put it upon Himself.

So Eliphaz was giving Job very unscriptural advice.

WAS JOB A HYPOCRITE?

Job's second friend was named Bildad, who accused him of being a hypocrite and a liar. As if it wasn't enough that Job's wife left him, his children were dead, his fortune was gone, and he's suffering in pain—Bildad topped that off by adding, "Oh, by the way, you're a two-faced phony!"

His so-called friend was asking Job to read between

the lines when he said, *"Behold, God will not cast away the blameless"* (Job 8:20).

It's almost always the mark of a betrayer when they come into your life; they will impugn your integrity, challenge your character, and question your motives. In truth, they're doing the work of the enemy of your soul.

The devil is called *"the accuser of [the] brethren"* (Revelation: 12:10).

Remember, these "comforters" are not Job's adversaries; they are his peers and confidants, friends who love him! They are wealthy men of the area that he socialized with and entertained in his home.

Now, however, when Job was at the lowest point in his life, he was expecting a helping hand up, but instead received a "neck step" with their boot which crushed him to the ground. Instead of being encouraged, he was being demoralized.

DID JOB DESERVE THIS?

Job's third and final friend was named Zophar.

This man proclaimed that Job's suffering was much less than what he had coming to him. Specifically, he said, *"God exacts from you less than your iniquity deserves"* (Job 11:6).

Are you kidding me? Job was physically sick,

mourning the loss of his family and wealth. I know many, who if they get one little splinter in their finger, think the world is coming to an end! But here's a God-fearing man who lost everything—including his dignity and standing in the community.

THREE PRINCIPLES

I wish I knew the answer to the question of why people are disloyal to their friends. I believe it is part of the wickedness of the human heart—and we are all guilty of breaking a trust at some level. Be careful of how swiftly you judge the betrayer, lest you find yourself walking in his shoes.

What I can do, however, is to equip you with some principles that will help you to overcome the betrayals in your life.

Principle #1: Only a friend is able to betray you because you would expect an enemy to act this way.

It's our nature to keep our enemies as far away as possible. We not only watch out for them, for protection we hide behind gates, walls, doors, and locks.

It is our friends who we greet with open arms and

invite inside the gates; they have access to the inner sanctum of our souls. This is why betrayal is so painful. It comes from a man or woman we loved and trusted.

There are individuals who make the mistake of keeping everybody at bay, of allowing no one access. I understand such reasoning and why we say, "It hurts so bad that I don't want to ever feel this way again, so I'm going to keep everybody on the other side of this wall."

In doing so you're sentencing yourself to a life of solitary confinement, of loneliness, and a bitter existence that ends in a cold, dark death.

While you cannot embrace and let everybody in, you must open the door to certain individuals. I know it's a scary thing, and you are reluctant to feel the knife of betrayal again, but you can't shut the whole world out.

Sociologists tell us that most well adjusted adults will have about 12 to 15 friends in their circle—people that they know and love on a somewhat personal level. Out of that number, they'll choose just two or three who will become best or intimate friends—people you would tell your whole life story to. These are individuals you would trust with your deepest darkest secret.

You need people in your life you can be real and honest with, putting it all on the table. These are individuals who can call you out, but you also know that they will love you *regardless,* and stand by your side.

Unfortunately, those are the ones who are also capable of letting you down, and I know it's a frightening position to be in. That's why someone wrote the song, "Love Hurts"—because it really does.

There's no heartache like the pain of love, yet there is no happiness like the joy of love. It a puzzle, a conundrum; the best of everything, but the worst of all. Yet we can't live without love!

In addition to two or three in your inner circle, and 12 to 15 friends that are close, outside that circle there are 75 to 100 acquaintances—people at work, in your neighborhood, clubs that you're a part of, or friendship circles you're connected with. So all in all, there are approximately 100 people in your life.

Jesus had a very similar set of circumstances. He had 70 volunteer staff members—preachers and leaders He was developing in ministry. Then He had the 12 disciples of His inner circle, the ones who traveled with Him, ministered with Him, and performed miracles. They were much like paid staff members.

From those 12, he had three—Peter, James, and John—who were His closest, most trusted friends.

Jesus' life was a picture of a healthy, adult human

being. His betrayer, Judas, however, came out of the inner circle.

Contrary to what some may say, I do not believe that Judas was predestined to be the betrayer. I say this because Judas had a free will, which God gives to every person who is born. He gifts us the power to choose, and we decide our own actions. The Lord may know the choices we are going to make, but He never forces us to make a decision.

FINALLY, SOME GOOD ADVICE

Even though Job's betrayers were friends and not enemies, there was a fourth man who came along in Job's story. His name was Elihu, and we find him toward the end of the book of Job.

Elihu offered some very sage advice. After hearing Job complain that even though he was innocent, God *"counts me as His enemy"* (Job 33:10), Elihu countered with, *"Why do you contend with Him? For He does not give an accounting of any of His words. For God may speak in one way, or in another, yet man does not perceive it"* (verses 13-14).

Notice that *He* and *Him* are capitalized, referring to Almighty God.

It is clear that the Lord doesn't have to justify His ways. According to Elihu, God may be explaining to us along the way, but we're just not getting the picture. We haven't grasped the fact that He declared, *"For as the heavens are higher than the earth, so are My ways higher than your ways, and My thoughts than your thoughts"* (Isaiah 55:9).

Maybe God is talking "big picture," yet all we can see is the immediate circumstance that surrounds us. Instead of seeing the larger view, we become lost in the details.

Principle #2: In the midst of betrayal, let God show you WHO He is.

Let me remind you that in days of darkness and pain there is going to be an opportunity for you to know the Shepherd more than you have ever known Him.

Most people are so distracted by their heartaches that they don't notice how close the Shepherd is to them. Some are so consumed with anger they won't even look His way!

In the dark days of your pain, do not waste all of your time and energy questioning why, but invest it on Who! Let Him show you who He is.

- Hold on tightly to His hand.
- Walk closely by His side.
- Listen intently to His voice.

- Press as closely as He will allow.
- Ask Him to carry you for awhile, and He will.

Don't be afraid to ask, "Will You hold me in Your arms, Shepherd? I'm scared. I'm alone and don't know what to do." Look up to Him and say, "Will You help me?"

The Shepherd will lift you from the pain of your darkness and carry you into the glory of His light. He may not ever (to your satisfaction) tell you *why,* but I promise you, He will show you *Who.*

What a gift that is!

THE ULTIMATE BETRAYAL

Jesus, just like you may have been, was betrayed by a friend. He could have stopped Judas from doing this to Him, because He knew it was coming. There are two prophecies in the Old Testament, authored by the Holy Spirit, that lets us know that Jesus knew this event was in His future—and He probably knew the culprit would be Judas. Yet, until the very last moment, Jesus called Judas, *"friend"* (Matthew 26:50).

Judas had an opportunity, even up to the final seconds, to change his mind, but he chose not to.

Can you imagine betraying Jesus Christ, the Son of God? Now in Judas' eyes, He was just a man. It seems as though he misunderstood the nature and character of God. But we now know that he was betraying the Almighty Himself.

Speaking of Jesus, John declared, *"He was in the world, and the world was made through Him"* (John 1:3). And Paul the Apostle wrote, *"All things were created through Him [Jesus] and for Him. And He is before all things, and in Him all things consist"* (Colossians 1:16-17).

At the moment of creation, it was Jesus, as part of the Godhead, who declared, "Let there be light."

- It was His voice that created the billions and billions of stars and galaxies in the night sky.
- With just the sound of His voice He brought into existence life on earth.
- He caused all of the plants, seeds, vegetables, and flowers to grow at His word.
- He ordered the sun and the moon and the earth to rotate.

It was the Son of God who created man out of dirt. He formed Adam's body, then breathed into his nostrils and man became a living soul. From that one exhale from the mouth of Jesus, Adam gave life to 14 billion people who have lived and died since creation—and seven billion are still living today.

He Understands What You are Going Through

How could a single solitary human being betray such a powerful Christ? I don't think Jesus was caught off guard. I believe He allowed it to happen because He wanted you to know what it's like to feel the sting of betrayal.

- When you cry about the pain of someone who has lost your trust, you can be certain He understands.
- When you tell Him about the suffering of your soul, He can identify.
- When you share with Him the anguish of your spirit, He knows exactly what you are saying.

Not only has Christ observed this, He lived it and bore it in His body and life.

Centuries before Christ came to earth, Zechariah the prophet spoke these words about the Lord's betrayal. *"If someone asks, 'What are these wounds on your body?' [referring to the Savior] they [Jesus] will answer, 'The wounds I was given at the house of my friends'"* (Zechariah 13:6 NIV).

That's what betrayal is.

Jesus and Judas were travel companions. They worked together, preached together, and prayed together. The Lord trusted His friend so much that He appointed him to be his chief financial officer, taking care of the money and paying the bills. This is how much faith Jesus had in Judas.

Yet when Jesus went to pray after the Last Supper, Judas told the soldiers and the officials from the Sanhedrin that he would walk out to the Garden of Gethsemane to show them which one was Jesus. *"Now His betrayer had given them a sign, saying, 'Whomever I kiss, He is the One; seize Him.' Immediately he went up to Jesus and said, 'Greetings, Rabbi!' and kissed Him"* (Matthew 26:48-49).

You only greet those you love or are close to with a kiss. You see, Judas had kissed Jesus many times as a friend. But on this occasion it was not an act of greeting, but one of betrayal.

Earlier, Matthew in his written account, had used Judas' name, but now he only refers to him as the *"betrayer."*

Have you ever been so upset at somebody that you wouldn't even utter his or her name? You refer to them as, "You know, the idiot." "Stupid guy." "The moron."

Judas was using his friendship right up to the very

end, calling Jesus "Rabbi" and kissing him.

It is incredible how Jesus responded. He simply asked Judas, *"Friend, why have you come?"* (verse 50).

I doubt I would have been so gracious. I probably would have been saying, "Put up your dukes, I'm about to take you out!"

BROTHERLY LOVE

Jesus modeled to us how we can win the victory over the betrayers in our life. It's not by becoming bitter, building a fort of protection, becoming a recluse, or cutting yourself off from society. No! That's the trick of the enemy and exactly what the evil one wants you to do. Satan's aim is to rob you of your relationships and faith.

Among the last words Judas heard from the Savior was "friend." In the Greek this is interpreted as *philos*. It's where Philadelphia gets it's name—The City of Brotherly Love.

I pray we will have the courage to love those who despitefully use us, and say, "I love you like a brother."

At that moment in the garden of Gethsemane, the Sanhedrin, priests, and Roman soldiers arrested Jesus, and you probably know the rest of the story. The Son of God was tried and convicted in two courts and sentenced to death on the cross.

Surely nothing good could possibly come from the betrayal of a friend. For three days it looked like Judas had won.

Today you may be facing your own Judas, your own betrayal. Or maybe you've been the disloyal friend. May I remind you that it's not the end of the story.

Principle #3: Only God can turn the darkness of your pain into the light of His love.

The noted writer C. S. Lewis is quoted as saying, "You will certainly carry out God's purpose, however you act. But it makes a difference to you whether you serve like Judas or like John."

We know what Judas was guilty of, he betrayed. Do you know what John did? He stood faithful till the end. He was the last disciple at Calvary, and was there when Christ died. All the others had walked away, but John stood at the foot of the cross watching Him shed His blood for you and me.

When Jesus, with a crown of thorns pressing upon His head, looked down and saw His mother, and John, the disciple he loved, standing there, He said to her, *"Woman, behold your son. Then he said to the disciple, 'Behold your mother!' And from that hour that disciple took her to his own home"* (John 19:26-27).

My question to you is: Who will you be? Will you be a Judas, or a John?

He's For You and With You!

Facing betrayal on your own can lead to months, years, even a lifetime of pain.

Tim Keller, pastor of the Redeemer Church in New York City, wrote these words: "Suffering is unbearable if you aren't certain that God is for you and with you."

I have personalized this for my own faith and continue to say, "God is for me, and God is with me."

Regardless of the situation, encourage yourself in the faith. Speak these words every day: God is for me, and God is with me.

Chapter 6

The Pain of Family

Nancy Mitford, a 20th century author, observed, "The great advantage of living in a large family is that it is an early lesson of life's essential unfairness."

Some feel that the larger the family, the greater the injustice.

It may be why, as youngsters, our moms do their best to teach us how to *share, give, forgive, love,* and *help each other.* All those things are intended to make us into the human beings we become as adults. But far too often we underestimate what we can learn from our families.

Let's be honest and admit up front that every family is a little dysfunctional. That's just the way we are. Now some of us have it more together than others, but every family is a little bit broken.

This being true, I want you to know that the hand of God is never prevented by the dysfunction of mankind. Our heavenly Father still works His will in us—even if we are part of a family that is flawed.

THE CHRONOLOGY

We have been looking at the life of Job, and his family certainly played a crucial part in the story.

The background of the account is fascinating. What we read in the book of Job takes place before the time of Abraham. Bible scholars aren't certain, but we can estimate that it was somewhere after the flood and before Abraham.

This means Job predates the Abrahamic Covenant of Faith, which was before the Covenant of Law that God made with Moses.

The events in the life of Job deal directly with Almighty God and a single human being—almost in isolation of other factors. In many respects it's just like *your* story—one between the Lord and you as an individual.

Perhaps this is why God chose to put Job first in the list of stories in the Bible. Of the 66 books in Scripture, each are filled with dozens of narratives, and Job comes first. You see, the Bible is not in chronological order. We who live in the Western hemisphere think chronologically. What time is it? What date is it? From one to ten, where is it placed? How old are you?

When's your birthday?

That's not true in the mindset of the Eastern hemisphere. There, it's more *event* driven. The focus is on the essence of life, not on the essence of time.

So the Bible was arranged in an Eastern mindset, which is a little different than the way we process facts in our world. So if you put the Bible in chronological order, Job would be placed near the beginning. Now we know it didn't take place before creation, but Moses was the author of the first five books of the Bible—Genesis, Exodus, Leviticus, Numbers, and Deuteronomy. In theological circles they are called the Pentateuch.

Genesis was handed down to Moses through oral tradition which he received from the Patriarchs. His forefathers related the stories, and Moses was the first to write them down under the inspiration of the Holy Spirit. He captured the accounts beginning at the moment of creation, the days of Joseph, and (in the book of Exodus) the miraculous liberation of the children of Israel from the bondage of Egypt.

In the next three books, Leviticus, Numbers, and Deuteronomy, Moses was giving a first hand account. With the exception of when he died and was buried, what Moses wrote happened to him personally, and he relates what God did in Israel during his lifetime.

What Was So Significant?

Since the events of Job take place before Moses wrote these five books, it only makes sense that what is placed at the start is usually the most important.

What was so significant about Job that God put his story first? Job is an apologetic book that deals primarily with faith. The word "apologetics" sounds like "apologize," but that is not its definition at all. It comes from a Greek root word which means "to defend the faith."

Someone who is an apologist or studies apologetics understands how to defend their belief system. There are preachers who are known for this. For example, Ravi Zechariah is a modern day apologist, and there were great ones in previous centuries including C. S. Lewis and G. K. Chesterton.

Every Christian should be at least a novice in apologetics to know how to defend his or her faith—and this is what the book of Job deals with.

It addresses the question of why people suffer—a topic we discussed earlier in this book. However, instead of giving a direct reply, it answers a different question. In the book of Job we are repeatedly brought back to this thought: whatever you are going through, the solution is to remain faithful to the Lord and to hold on to your faith.

It may be that we are given this answer because we cannot understand the circumstances of negative events that happen to us. Perhaps if God told us, we wouldn't get it, like it, or even be able to process the facts. Maybe it's too far outside of our ability to comprehend.

So, in the 42 chapters of Job, the Almighty gives us the best answer: no matter what you are enduring in your life today, never lose your trust in the Lord and cling tightly to your faith.

Does Job grow hopeless during his ordeal? Yes. He becomes despondent and even protests the injustice of his circumstances. But during all the chaos and calamity, Job chooses to remain faithful and trust the Lord.

Allow me to be transparent and confess that there have been times on my journey of faith where I have protested to the Lord concerning injustices and situations that have come my way.

However, I have learned that God already knows what's in our hearts. When we are doubting, it's better to say out loud, "Hey God, I don't get this. I don't know why You're doing this, and I don't really like what's taking place. But I'm going to trust and serve You anyway."

Whatever you're facing at this very moment, the best thing you can do is to come to terms with the circumstances, knowing that the toughest conflict will always be fought on the battlefield of faith.

Your Most Valuable Resource

The story of Job is also yours—a person who fights daily for his faith. If I asked whether or not you have faced such a struggle in the past six months, what would be your answer?

Having waves of doubt is understandable because we are human beings—people living on earth, trying to grasp in our clay hands this eternal treasure called faith. It is, *"the substance of things hoped for, the evidence of things not seen"* (Hebrews 11:1).

Today, you may not understand or have a true sense of your faith's worth, but it is your most valuable resource.

On a scale of 1 to 10, how important is your faith? Is it a 1, a 5, or a 10? Is it something you hold onto only when it's easy, or do you tenaciously cling to it no matter what?

Like gravity, faith can't be seen and you cannot touch or feel it, but we know that everything rests on its pull. Without gravity, you wouldn't be reading this book right now—you'd be floating somewhere in outer space!

No one knows what makes gravity work, yet we know that without it, life on this planet could not exist.

The same is true in the spiritual world of faith. We can't see it, touch it, taste it, or feel it, but you know you can't live without it.

Job protested to the Lord the injustice of his life, but the Bible says that he chose to remain faithful through everything and trust the Lord. I also want to remind you that Scripture states, *"In all this Job did not sin with his lips"* (Job 2:10).

So it must not be sinful to have a conversation with God when you're having doubts about your faith. The Lord already knows your apprehensions and fears, but it's perfectly permissible to say it out loud: "Hey God, I'm doubting!"

It's Okay to Question

In the New Testament we are told of a blind man who was brought to Jesus at Bethsaida, begging the Lord to touch him. The Bible describes how Jesus *"took the blind man by the hand and led him out of the town. And when He had spit on his eyes and put His hands on him, He asked him if he saw anything. And he looked up and said, 'I see men like trees, walking'"* (Mark 8:23-24).

It's okay to vocalize when things aren't as they should be. In this case, Jesus not only listened, He *"put His hands on his eyes again and made him look up. And he was restored and saw everyone clearly"* (verse 25).

There was another occasion where the distraught father of a demon-possessed boy approached Jesus, pleading, *"If you can do anything, have compassion on us and help us"* (Mark 9:22).

Jesus told him, *"If you can believe, all things are possible to him who believes. Immediately the father of the child cried out and said with tears, "Lord, I believe; help my unbelief!"* (verses 23-24).

We must be honest and put it all on the table. Acknowledge where you really are in the process and say, "Father, help me to finish this story."

Job's entire account is told in the context of his family, his friends, and his God.

We get into trouble when we stubbornly say, "I'm going to do it my way." The Lord will let you, but you'll find yourself in a mess so quickly that you won't even know what hit you.

Job's ordeal is being played out in the arena of his marriage, his children, his best friends, and his Creator. It's also the canvas on which our story is painted.

Often, however:

- We become so focused on the canvas God has given us that we forget to paint.
- We become so focused on the paper that we forget to write the song.
- We become so focused on the troubles that we forget to live life.

Time is precious. We must not let life pass us by, centering on only what's wrong. Live each day to the fullest and trust that God is going to see you through.

A Transformational Agent

The details of Job's personal life are more than interesting. He was married to his wife for many years, several decades at least, maybe much longer. He was a patriarch and probably lived hundreds of years, so his marriage may have also lasted that long. He was the father of ten children, ran a successful business, had at least three close friends, and enjoyed a very intimate relationship with the Lord.

But as we see, it's the pain inside of our relationships that becomes the transformational agent of our lives.

- You may think that God placed you in a family that is ruining you.
- You may think that God has given you friends who have betrayed you.
- You may think that God has forgotten or forsaken you.

I guarantee if you remain faithful to the Lord, you have a valued place in His eternal plan.

Never forget that Job was *"blamless and upright, and one who feared God and shunned evil"* (Job 1:1). Simply put, he was a *good* man who had a *good* heart, and did *good* things.

I don't want you to miss the fact that Job wasn't just one of the most heralded individuals of his day, the Bible tells us, *"...this man was the greatest of all the people of the East"* (verse 3). He was famous, rich, powerful, and influential. By today's standards, if Job were living on a ranch in Texas he'd have 12 thousand head of cattle and be prosperous beyond most of our wildest dreams. He'd have a large paid staff and a booming business.

But Job lived more than 5,000 years ago, so in that economy he was probably a *multi-billionaire.*

In that environment, God was working on Job. One of the lessons we can apply is that the Lord uses imperfect families to shape and mold us.

Today, many think their family is the problem, but God uses damaged relationships to work His way in us.

Guess who is the problem—*we* are!

The more time and attention you place on your parents, brothers, sisters, or your neighbors, the less time you're going to allow God to work on you.

The only person in this world that you can change is YOU! No matter what others do, you can choose to allow the Holy Spirit to finish His work on the inside. Though it may not seem like it, God placed you with the right people at the right time in the right place. The only question to answer is this, "Will you remain faithful to the Lord, and love your family regardless of their shortcomings?

I fully understand that there are degrees of dysfunction, but I also firmly believe that the flawed, maladjusted condition of man cannot negate the effectiveness of God. The Almighty can do a work in you—in any situation.

Even though families are often less than perfect, they are the classroom of life where we learn much of what we need to know. Either someone will teach you or you will learn by observing the wrong behavior.

I understand that many of us live in painful situations, and I don't want to discount or underestimate this. But I want you to remember that God is with you—and there really are positive things taking place in your family. So what may cause us the most pain can bring us the most joy.

In the midst of it all we find the transforming hand of God working deep in our spirit to shape us into the image of Christ.

What Will Be Your Response?

Job made a crucial decision. Even though his world crumbled around his feet, he clung tightly to his faith. The Bible tells us, *"Then Job arose, tore his robe, and shaved his head; and he fell to the ground and worshiped"* (Job 1:20).

Then he made this profound statement: *"Naked I came from my mother's womb, and naked shall I return there. The Lord gave, and the Lord has taken away; blessed be the name of the Lord"* (verse 21).

When our time of testing comes, whether we lose a little, a lot, or *everything* like Job, what will be our response? Will we fall to the ground and worship? Will we bless the name of Almighty God?

Regardless of the level of your pain, little, much, or too great to bear, hold on to your faith—and never let it go!

CHAPTER 7

THE PAIN OF DISCIPLINE

Boxing champion Mohamed Ali once said, "When I'm doing sit-ups I don't even start counting them until it hurts, because up until that time they don't really count anyway."

What a powerful example of the pain of discipline!

We are trained from an early age to avoid anything that "hurts," and wisely so. We're taught to look both ways before crossing a street, to wear a helmet when we ride our bikes, etc. But the pain of discipline is unique, in that it is a beneficial discomfort that transforms us.

I recently read the inspiring book, *The Heavenly Man,* written by Brother Yun, an underground church leader in China. In the introduction by co-author Paul Hattaway was this quote: "It's not great men who changed the world but weak men in the hands of a great God."

Do you know why the Lord uses weak people? It's

because, in reality, they are the only ones available! When we understand our frailties, it is a sign of spiritual maturity, and knowledge is gained only after we realize how little we really know. It is at this point where wisdom can flow into our lives.

Whether we have acknowledged it or not, we are all completely dependent on the Lord—for the air we breathe and the water we drink. These resources are not a gift from the government, but from above. Only God could create oxygen and none other than the Almighty can sustain life.

We depend on the Lord, not only for our physical being, but for our spiritual existence.

As we study the life of Job, we have a clear picture of how God uses the pain of discipline to transform us.

However, we need to understand that sometimes our attempts at spiritual discipline are not born out of pure motives. I've met those who say all the right words and display a spiritual image for fleshly reasons. For example, some try to look "holy" in an effort to impress those around them. Others exhibit a pious attitude, trying to attract the Lord's love and acceptance.

These are impure motives because God couldn't love you any more than He already does. In addition, what others think of us is immaterial because our worth comes from the Creator not from the creation. It is God Himself who gives us value.

Awesome Attributes

Let me share four healthy traits of spiritual discipline:

One: Healthy spiritual discipline should be founded on God's love.

You cannot advance one step in your walk with the Lord until you understand the truth that God is totally in love with you. He knows your name, your thoughts, and the intents of your heart.

As I like to say:

- If God had a refrigerator your picture would be on it.
- If God had a night stand, your photo would be in a frame.
- If God had a wallet, your picture would be the first one shown.
- If God had a smartphone, you'd be in His photo app.

Your heavenly Father loves you desperately, and

until you have that revelation etched on your heart, nothing else is going to make sense.

The Lord doesn't love you *if,* or, *when,* or *because.* He loves you, *period!*

The only proper motivation toward discipline is to understand how much God deeply cares for you; therefore allowing Him to change you.

Two: Healthy spiritual discipline is focused on growing in grace.

The grace of God is the supernatural ability to finish tasks and objectives that you're not capable of doing on your own. The Lord fills in the gap and makes up the difference.

However, healthy discipline is not centered on begging God to give you grace, rather it is walking in the grace He has already provided.

Even though you feel you are falling short, in His eyes you are still sufficient, accepted, loved, and made whole because of God's unmerited favor—grace. This is the cornerstone of your spiritual growth.

Three: Healthy spiritual discipline produces the character of Christ.

The reason you should seek and practice spiritual discipline is because, in the process, the Holy Spirit is working in your life, filling you with the attributes of Christ. He is forming you into His image.

What does it mean to have the character of Christ? They are listed as the fruit of the Spirit, and include, *"love, joy, peace, longsuffering, kindness, goodness, faithfulness, gentleness, [and] self-control"* (Galatians 5:22-23).

These are provided by the Holy Spirit and serve to help you become more like the Savior.

Four: Healthy spiritual discipline opens the door to new spiritual gifts.

Every believer is given at least one (if not more) spiritual gift. You may not know what yours is, or even have used what the Lord has graciously blessed you with, but it's there inside you, waiting to be released.

We know this is true because Scripture tells us, *"the manifestation of the Spirit is given to each one for the profit of all"* (1 Corinthians 12:7), and *"the same Spirit works all these things, distributing to each one individually as He wills"* (verse 11).

Be encouraged. You possess one of these gifts, even if you haven't yet discovered, developed, or put it into practice.

There are many spiritual gifts. For example, *"to one is given the word of wisdom through the Spirit, to another the word of knowledge through the same Spirit, to another faith by the same Spirit, to another gifts of healings by the same Spirit, to another the working of miracles, to another prophecy, to another discerning of spirits, to another different kinds of tongues, to another the interpretation of tongues"* (verses 8-10).

What if I purchased a bicycle for you today and you wheeled it home but, not knowing how to ride it, you parked it in your garage? You own a bicycle but you are not a cyclist because you are not using your gift. You have to roll that bike out of the garage, climb on, place your feet on the pedals, put your legs in motion, and practice your skills.

There may be a few unexpected tumbles and falls along the way. You'll probably scrape your elbow or your knee, perhaps even crashing your bike in the learning process. The secret to success is that when you fall down, you get back up and continue riding down the path.

Whatever your spiritual gift may be, allow the Spirit to identify and develop it within you. You probably won't master its use at first, and are not likely to be proficient for months or even years, but as you faithfully practice, you become an extension of God's hand in the earth.

Spiritual Discipline in Action

Allow me to share a story about a young man I met not long ago. At the age of 17, he was living in Alexandria, Louisiana, and had grown up in a really rough neighborhood.

He became a product of his environment and was soon involved in drugs and crime, and one day accidentally killed a person. The young man was arrested, accused of manslaughter, tried, found guilty, and received a long sentence—up to life in prison.

He was incarcerated in Louisiana's Angola Prison for over 19 years, with little or no hope of being released.

However, during this time, he gave his heart to Christ, was water baptized, received the infilling of the Holy Spirit, enrolled in seminary, earned his bachelors degree in theological studies, and began the process of being a credentialed minister.

The warden at Angola, one of the most godly men I've ever met, asked this inmate to be the pastor of the church in Angola, and he became in charge of the weekly prison chapel. Hundreds of the most hardened criminals came voluntarily on Sunday mornings to hear him preach God's Word. Even the warden attended the services and called him, "my pastor."

Through a series of divine events God did something amazing in this man's life. In a hearing before the parole board, he was granted release after almost 20 years behind bars.

Here's an individual who submitted himself to painful spiritual discipline while facing life in prison. Yet I've met men and women on the other end of the spectrum. They have complete freedom, but refuse to yield themselves to God's calling.

How often has the enemy distracted you from your destiny by making you look at your circumstances? Are you still pursuing your spiritual gifts?

The pain of discipline is doing what is ethical and right, even when everything appears to be hopeless. It can unlock doors that no man can open. What if the prisoner I mentioned had somehow been paroled, but never received his seminary degree or committed himself to Christian service? Who knows what would have become of him. But now he has the opportunity to bring the Gospel to every person he has met in the past, and those he will touch in the future.

SPEAKING PERSONALLY

I've been asked, "Doug, what are the spiritual

disciplines that have influenced your life?" There have been many, but let me share four that have not only impacted my past, but I still practice them today.

First: Fasting and prayer

Each January we start our church year with 21 days of fasting and prayer. Personally, I have done this annually since I was 16 years old.

Fasting, limiting your food intake and denying yourself, is a transformational discipline that the Holy Spirit can use mightily in your life. It takes the focus off self and turns your thoughts toward God's will and His purposes.

When fasting is combined with prayer, it produces power beyond description. Prayer is not some spiritual exercise you become involved with because your minister tells you that you should. It's also a mistake to pray like someone else, repeating their words. Prayer should flow from your inner being and be an ongoing conversation with God.

Second: Study the Word of God

You may attend church on Sunday morning and listen to a 40 minute message, but there's no way you can sustain your spiritual life on one sermon a week and remain a healthy Christian. Would you eat only one meal every seven days?

Well, your spiritual man is the same. It is impossible to maintain your spiritual energy level without the right input. However, a pastor's job is not to spoon-feed you; it is to show you where the food is so you can daily feed yourself. There are countless versions of the Bible at your fingertips—plus online commentaries, concordances, and study guides that will provide you with amazing biblical knowledge.

The reason I emphasize, "study the Word of God," is because those who don't will spiritually starve to death!

Third: Worship

I married a worshiper. Rachel is not just a singer or only a worship leader, she is a worshiper all the time, everywhere we go. I love this about her because she challenges me to reach the next level. Recently, as we were driving down the highway and the radio was cranking out some country music, she turned to me and said, "Really? Can't we get into some praise and worship?"

Let me encourage you to enter the throne room where Jesus is. The door to heaven is opened through worship.

I pray your love for the Lord will not only find

expression in your thoughts, but in your voice. If you are a new believer and aren't sure what to say, or how, open the pages of the book of Psalms. You will discover powerful words of praise, worship, and inspiration.

You can echo the psalmist and say, *"Whom have I in heaven but You? And there is none upon earth that I desire besides You. My flesh and my heart fail; but God is the strength of my heart and my portion forever"* (Psalm 73:25-26).

Worship is a spiritual experience without compare.

Fourth: Serve others

This includes offering to do a job that no one else may want to, and serving when you're not in the spotlight.

When Christ has His rightful place in our daily lives, His Lordship will be demonstrated in the way we minister and help others. As Jesus told the disciples, *"If anyone desires to be first, he shall be last of all and servant of all"* (Mark 9:35).

POSITIVE PARALLELS

The four spiritual disciplines that have been central to my Christian walk, are not new or unique. In fact, they parallel those found in the life of Job:

Number 1: Job was a man of prayer.

How do we know Job prayed? In his own words he looked up to God and cried, "*Remember, I pray, that You have made me like clay. And will You turn me into dust again?*" (Job 10:9).

In this heartfelt prayer, Job acknowledged that God was Sovereign and that if He so chose He could end his life.

Number 2: Job loved God's Word.

Here was a person who knew the law of the Almighty. He declared, *"I have not departed from the commandment of His lips; I have treasured the words of His mouth more than my necessary food"* (Job 23:12).

Now that's being in love with God's Word!

Here in south Louisiana we'd say it like this: "I treasure His Word more than my crawfish étouffée, more than jambalaya, gumbo, or fried catfish!"

If you can make a comparison with something you enjoy, you're on the right track.

Number 3: Job was a worshiper of the Almighty.

Job didn't lift his praises toward heaven or play an

instrument just for show or accolades; it was because he wanted to tell God how much he loved Him.

Immediately after the messenger arrived bearing the terrible news that Job's children had been killed, his cattle destroyed, and all his possessions wiped out, Scripture records, *"Then Job arose, tore his robe, and shaved his head; and he fell to the ground and worshiped"* (Job 1:20).

Worship is the most intimate spiritual experience you can have with Almighty God. As I recently told my congregation, "Worship is to the spirit what sex is to the body." In spiritual worship, there is a relief and pleasure that is unexplainable. The Bible calls it *"joy unspeakable"* (1 Peter 1:8 KJV).

It is mind-boggling, but mysteries will be revealed to the worshiper that otherwise they have no way of knowing. It is the greatest high, yet it's an addiction that is free. It is one that will forever transform your life and has no damaging side effects!

Number 4: Job was a humble servant.

Let's be realistic. You're not going to pray, fast, read the Bible, and worship 24 hours a day. But there is one thing you should always find the time for, and it is to humbly serve those around you.

Remember, God considered Job to be an unpretentious servant who lived a blameless, upright life. He told Satan, *"Have you considered My servant Job, that there is none like him on the earth...?"* (Job 1:8).

Job faithfully and humbly served his God, his wife, his family, his business, and his customers. Perhaps this is why he was called *"the greatest of all the people of the East"* (verse 3).

There may not be a higher compliment that God could ever grace you with than for Him to call you, "My servant."

In His own words, Jesus said, *"...the Son of Man did not come to be served, but to serve"* (Matthew 20:28).

He also taught this as a principal to His disciples, letting them know that the highest in God's kingdom would be whoever serves the most.

This is polar opposite to what most people think. They believe the number one leader or potentate gives orders and has his own hired hands. But in the kingdom of God, the servant is the ruler!

A true servant, without complaining, picks the hardest job and the toughest tasks. What's more, he will do it out of the limelight when no one else notices, purely for the joy of serving.

A young man was on our staff for about a year and a half before he and his family went to Argentina to be missionaries. I've known him for many years.

While he was with us, finishing seminary, and becoming credentialed and appointed to his missionary position, he didn't sit around twiddling his thumbs, but sweated and worked while he waited.

When our church was creating a "prayer walk," he was the individual who did the "grunt" work, digging a large hole, pouring the concrete, and helping to erect a large cross on the site.

His servant's heart was visible to all and I knew without a doubt that he would make a tremendous impact in foreign lands for God's glory.

Now it's Your Turn

Let me challenge you to perform a self-diagnostic. Right now, prayerfully examine your heart to see what spiritual discipline requires your immediate attention. Of the four listed below, which one has the Holy Spirit prompted to be activated in your life?

- Is it prayer and fasting? Maybe God is calling you to renew your commitment in these areas.
- Is it studying God's Word? Perhaps it is time to join a small group Bible study or be involved in a discipleship class.

- Is it worship? Enter into praise the moment it begins in your church. Raise your hands and your voice to the Lord. But never limit your worship to just Sundays, lift up the Lord every day of the week
- Is it serving? Join the servant leaders team of the congregation. This is your opportunity to minister side-by-side with fellow believers.

When you yield your gifts, your talents, and *yourself* totally to the Lord, you'll find that spiritual discipline is far from being a pain; it is a God-blessed, heaven-sent pleasure.

Chapter 8

The Pain of Change

There's one question that has been debated by philosophers and scientists on university campuses for decades: What would happen if an immovable object were confronted with an unstoppable force?

No matter how hard great minds try, they can't seem to find a solution to this puzzle. The answer they usually come up with is, "Because of the laws of physics, two things cannot exist in the same place. You'll either have one or the other because eventually one will win."

Even though this is a philosophical discussion, we are watching this quandary play out across the American landscape.

Our culture is the unstoppable force, and it is running on a collision course with the Bible, which is the immovable object.

My question is, who will win this battle? Will society be victorious, or God's Word?

You probably know my bias. I am risking my whole life on the Bible—and I'm putting my money where my mouth is! I am not trusting in the culture, but on the infallible Word of God.

Let me tell you why I have such confidence in the Bible. It has survived every kingdom and government known to man, and has thrived to this very day. Scripture, inspired by the Holy Spirit, has lived through the Egyptian empire, the Meads, Persians, Babylonians, Greeks, Romans, the Dark Ages, even the Soviet Union. Right now, Scripture is alive and well, flourishing underground in Communist China.

I can assure you that the Word of God will also outlast the American Empire. This is why I want you to know that in a changing world, put your hope in God's unchanging Word. It was written so that we could have a personal relationship with Jesus Christ, whom the Father sent to earth: *"And the Word became flesh and dwelt among us"* (John 1:14).

THREE "CHANGE" PRINCIPLES

The clashes between culture and Christianity have only begun. Removing prayer from school classrooms was just the start. We are seeing atheistic legislation in the name of political correctness weaken the pillars of a nation that was founded on Jedeo-Christian principles.

Since transformation is usually associated with pain, we need to see things from heaven's perspective. Even in the midst of moral and social revolution, God has tremendous plans for His children—and much of it involves change.

Please allow me to share these three important facts:

Principle #1: Some things never change.

Christ Jesus has been here *from* everlasting—and He will be here *until* everlasting: from eternity to eternity. He exists outside of time and space. He is the Alpha and the Omega, the beginning and the end. He's the first and the last and He remains steadfast. How do we know this? Because the Bible tells us, *"Jesus Christ is the same yesterday, today, and forever"* (Hebrews 13:8).

While Jesus always loved the sinner, He did not hesitate to confront sin. As the church, we can do no less.

We also hold to the truth that the Bible is the infallible Word of God. We know it is without error and that the major translations we currently have are accurate because, basically, they do not vary from the texts that date back nearly 2,000 years. Almost every book in the Old Testament has an ancient copy that still exists and we can, with confidence, know that the Bible translated today is just like it was at the time of Christ.

The 27 books of the New Testament are also the Word of God. Combining the Old Covenant with the New, these 66 books written on three continents by 40 different authors in three different languages still stand as God's holy Word. As Jesus declared, *"Heaven and earth will pass away, but my words will by no means pass away"* (Matthew 24:35).

Never place your hope in the culture of man, but in the Word of God.

The Bible is nearly one-third prophecy, most of it pertaining to the last days. A great portion of it spoken by Jesus Himself and by His disciples, in particular John, who wrote the entire book of Revelation as a picture of the end times.

Of the hundreds of prophecies recorded in the Bible, many have been fulfilled, some are currently unfolding, and I believe the rest will take place in our generation.

Here are three prophecies that will affect your eternity:

First: Jesus is coming back soon.

Scripture tells of the prophetic signs of the times, when *"you will hear wars and rumors of wars...nation will rise against nation. And there will be famines, pestilences, and earthquakes"* (Matthew 24: 6-7).

The next event on God's agenda is the rapture of the church: *"For the Lord Himself will descend from heaven with a shout, with the voice of an archangel, and with the trumpet of God. And the dead in Christ will rise first. Then we who are alive and remain shall be caught up together with them in the clouds to meet the Lord in the air. And thus we shall always be with the Lord"* (1 Thessalonians 4:16-17).

Second: After Christ returns there will be a Great Tribulation upon the earth like the world has never seen.

This is when the false prophet and the antichrist will rise up and people will be required to take the mark of the beast. *"He causes all, both small and great, rich and poor, free and slave, to receive a mark on their right hand or on their foreheads, and that no one may buy or sell except one who has the mark or the name of the beast, or the number of his name"* (Revelation 13:16-17).

Plans for this are being made at this very moment. There is a strategy in development by the United Nations to number every person on the planet. There is discussion about testing this on newborn babies by inserting a digital chip, of all places, on the back of their hand or on their forehead.

That sounds like the Bible to me!

Third: After your earthly death there will be a day of judgment.

Every person on earth—sinner, saint, pauper, potentate, *"shall give account of himself to God"* (Romans 14:12). There are no exceptions: *"For we must all appear before the judgment seat of Christ"* (2 Corinthians 5:10).

The decision is yours. Are you going to live according to the culture, or in agreement with God's Word?

Principle #2: Some things need to change.

When I was a first grader in public school, at the beginning of each day, we said the Pledge of Allegiance and our teacher prayed over us in Jesus' name. If this was done today, the teacher would be put in jail!

In the last half-century, there has been a slow, steady transformation of our society. Month-to-month, we may not notice it, but in comparison with just a few decades ago, the change is drastic. Perhaps we need to pay attention to the second law of thermodynamics—that everything tends towards chaos.

Human life itself is decomposing in slow motion—almost like time-lapsed photography. This shouldn't surprise us, especially when we read what the Apostle Paul told the believers in Corinth: *"...this world in its present form is passing away"* (1 Corinthian 7:31 NIV).

There is only one hope, the church and the message of the Gospel. As believers, Christ is in us, performing the ministry of reconciliation—reconciling the world to Him.

Since the days are numbered, it is imperative that we bring the message of salvation to all nations and cultures. Because of incredible advances in technology, linguistic experts and theologians are working together to translate the Scriptures into every known language on the planet. We've never been able to say that before.

The implications are enormous. Over 2,000 years ago, when Jesus was being held captive under Roman rule and was given a death sentence, He made this incredible statement: *"This gospel of the kingdom will be preached in all the world as a witness to all the nations, and then the end will come"* (Matthew 24:14).

At that moment in time, Christ followers did not travel outside Israel. It was unthinkable to carry the message to the Middle East or Europe, let alone Asia or Africa. But now His words are being fulfilled. That's why we still send missionaries and teams around the globe. When the church finishes her assignment, Jesus is returning to claim His own. When will it happen? Christ stated, *"But of that day and hour no one knows, not even the angels of heaven, but My Father only"* (verse 36).

There will come a day when God tells His Son, "Go get My people." At that instant, the church will be taken from this earth. Can you imagine this world without the body of Christ? It will decay into debauchery and sin and be ruled by the antichrist. It will be a time of unprecedented tribulation. Then the final judgment.

This is why sharing the Gospel with *everyone* is so urgent.

Something else will take place in the last days. The church will fall under enormous persecution—and we see it happening at this very moment in nation after nation. Jesus said, *"If the world hates you, you know that it hated Me before it hated you...If they persecuted Me, they will also persecute you"* (John 15:18,20).

Society is not going to celebrate Christians or give us trophies, but will do everything in its power to arrest pastors, close churches, and persecute believers.

THE GRAND RECEPTION!

Now for the *good* news! While all of this is transpiring, God promises, *"And it shall come to pass in the last days...that I will pour out of My Spirit on all flesh"* (Acts 2:17).

The church will never be defeated. She is the Bride of Christ and will spend eternity in heaven with Jesus. When the rapture takes place, the world will be plunged into the Great Tribulation. But as the church, you and I will be at the Marriage Supper of the Lamb, being united with Jesus. You don't want to miss this glorious reception!

So instead of worrying or wringing your hands over the downward spiral of America, think about the awesome plans your heavenly Father has for you! Rejoice in the fact that if the Bible says it, that settles it—and the Word of God will last forever.

Principle #3: There is only one thing that I can change.

I've finally come to the conclusion that I alone can't change the world. I can't even change my spouse, and Lord knows I've tried! What's more, she can't alter me—because I'm too stubborn!

The only thing I can change, is *myself.* But to accomplish this, I need help. And this is where the power of the Holy Spirit comes in.

Without question, transformation is painful:

- It means I have to give up what I like.
- It means I have to give up my way and what I want.
- It means I have to give up my opinion and what I think.

The bottom line is that I must allow God to have total control of my thoughts and desires. As Paul wrote, *"May God himself, the God of peace, sanctify you through and through. May your whole spirit, soul and body be kept blameless at the coming of our Lord Jesus Christ"* (1 Thessalonians 5:23 NIV).

This is a fundamental theological building block. To know how to change, you need to understand how you are made. You are one person but you have three distinct parts. Like the Trinity is Father, Son and Holy Spirit (three in one), you too are a triune being—body, soul, and spirit. And the three are housed in one person.

THE "SOUL" CHANGE

Most of us have trouble with transformation because we are trying to change the wrong part of us. We think it's either a spiritual issue or a fleshly one, but in essence it is neither: it is a *soul* change.

The work God is doing in us is taking place at a very deep level—whether we have been saved five days or five decades.

When you accept Christ, at that instant of conversion you spirit is redeemed. You become a new person: Jesus called it being "born again." You are sealed with the spirit of Christ and you are redeemed. If you were to die at that moment you would go to be with Jesus. We know this is true because Jesus turned to the repentant thief hanging on the cross next to Him, uttering the words, *"Today you will be with Me in Paradise"* (Luke 23:43).

After conversion, your battle is not in your flesh—because you're never going to win that fight. Instead, *"Those who are Christ's have crucified the flesh with its passions and desires"* (Galatians 5:24).

We make a terrible mistake when we adapt the Gospel to make people feel better about themselves. Instead, they need to feel guilty about their sin so that they will repent and live according to how God designed them.

After your spirit is redeemed, your body will become new, then comes the hard part: your soul needs to be changed. That is what you and I all struggle with.

The word "soul" derives from the Greek word *psychi,* which is where we get the English term "psyche."

The Apostle Paul is saying that we are body, soul, and spirit (1 Thessalonians 5:23). As soul, we are a psychological person. And this is where the battle rages, in our minds—those six inches of space between our ears!

That being said, Paul counsels us further: *"Therefore, I urge you, brothers and sisters, in view of God's mercy, to offer your bodies as a living sacrifice, holy and pleasing to God—this is your true and proper worship. Do not conform to the pattern of this world, but be transformed by the renewing of your mind. Then you will be able to test and approve what God's will is—his good, pleasing and perfect will"* (Romans 12:1-2 NIV).

This is not a casual reminder, but "I URGE YOU" to heed the lesson!

In these two verses, written to believers, instead of mentioning our spirit (which is already redeemed) Paul addresses the body and soul (mind)—what we see, touch, and think. This is where the battle is ongoing! Basically, the apostle is letting us know that unless your body is a slave to Christ, you will be a slave to sin. Which will you choose?

It's in the renewing of your mind that you are able to test and prove what God's will is for YOU!

Your thought life is more than significant; it is vital. Scripture tells us that as a man *"thinks in his heart, so is he"* (Proverbs 27:3). This may explain why the pain of change is so real, because it's being fought in your mind. Since thoughts conceive lust, and you no longer want it to control your behavior, you have to alter the way you think.

Please, with God's help, make a commitment to stop giving your thought life ideas and images that lead you into sin. Oh, I can tell you to put a filter on your Internet and a long list of "don'ts," but rules rarely work. If you are in doubt regarding whether you should look at a particular website, watch that movie, or read a certain book, ask the Holy Spirit. He will guide you.

Your carnal thoughts give birth to fear and before you know it, you are paralyzed because you're afraid of a negative outcome. The economy may collapse, the bank systems may fail, and your future could be in jeopardy.

We all seek security, solace, and peace, but the only true Comforter is the Holy Spirit.

Sadly, our thoughts exert their own will, but as fully devoted followers of God's Son, we are called to surrender everything to Him.

"Let this mind be in you which was also in Christ Jesus" (Philippians 2:5). It's the only path to lasting change.

CHAPTER 9

THE PAIN OF EMOTION

Rachel and I were married in 1981. This was before cable television was widely available. We owned a 12-inch black-and-white TV set that only received one channel at night. So we would gather close to the screen and watch reruns of the original *Star Trek* with Captain Kirk and Mr. Spock—an alien who suppressed all of his emotions.

I've met people much like Spock. They put a lid on their feelings, and have a difficult time relating to others.

When God made you, He placed in you the gift of emotions so you can feel what it's like to be a human being. Without this, you'd be just a zombie.

British playwright/philosopher Oscar Wilde made this astute observation: "I don't want to be at the mercy of my emotions. I want to use them, to enjoy them, and to dominate them."

Mr. Wilde wasn't a theologian, but as we will learn this mirrors what we find in God's Word.

Personally, I'm an emotional being and enjoy a good cry. My wife and I will watch a movie we've seen ten times, and I know in advance when my tears will start flowing. Rachel thinks I'm ridiculous, and tries to keep me balanced, but I'm well prepared, with the popcorn and Kleenex at hand!

To be honest, I love to feel emotions, and be moved to the core. For example, if I find a video of a good comedian, I will watch his routine over and over, laughing myself silly.

THE FOUR FACTORS OF FEELINGS

There is a long list of emotions, but sociologists tell us our feelings can be categorized into these four:

Emotion #1: Happiness
If there's one thing every person on earth is pursuing, it is the desire to be happy.

In the story of Job, even though he found himself in a sad situation, he wished those around him were happy. His friends were mocking him and making fun of his faith and his walk with God, but he was secure enough to allow others to laugh at him. At one point Job said, *"Yet my friends laugh at me, for I call on God and expect an answer. I am a just and blameless man, yet they laugh at me"* (Job 12:4 NLT).

It is a mark of maturity when you can withstand ridicule, even seeing some humor in it all. Our first response is usually to defend or explain ourselves. We feel the need to justify our frailties, but Job embraced his. He remarked, *"People who are at ease mock those in trouble. They give a push to people who are stumbling"* (verse 5).

He is pointing out that his friends were overdoing their scorn, receiving pleasure from his pain. However, he did not respond with the self-defense mechanism that many of us are trapped in. Instead, he stated, *"But robbers are left in peace, and those who provoke God live in safety—though God keeps them in his power"* (verse 6).

His point being: we must not allow other people's scorn to rock our world.

A Merry Heart

Happiness is a choice. It's not going to show up on your front porch with a suitcase in hand and stay awhile. You see, true happiness is not a byproduct of people, things, or money. You can buy a lot of "stuff" in your search for enjoyment, but it never gets to the core problem. This is why I constantly preach, "What people should seek is to be right with Jesus, because He is the source of pure joy and happiness."

Let me share a practical tool. This may sound rather foolish, but when I was young and reached the ice cream section at the grocery store, I would skip up and down the aisle with excitement, and it would always bring a smile to my face—and to those who saw my playfulness. In fact, when our kids were small and they would be down in the dumps, I'd ask them, "Okay, who wants to go to the store and skip down the ice cream aisle?" They were always ready, and it changed their outlook. Of course, I also had to buy them some ice cream!

The ability to laugh has a way of healing your soul. Perhaps this is why the Bible tells us, *"A merry heart does good, like medicine"* (Proverbs 17:22). It makes you healthy and whole!

There will be times when you don't feel like it, but learn to laugh at yourself, and with others—even if you don't get the joke! Smile often, as much as you possibly can.

In all situations and circumstances, remember, *"The joy of the Lord is your strength"* (Nehemiah 8:10).

and toes while making their way to the top. I thought about that when I read, *"...do not give the devil a foothold"* (Ephesians 4:27 NIV).

If you give the enemy the smallest opportunity, he will get into your imagination, whisper in your ears, poison all of your relationships, and climb into your soul. Why? Because we fail to take control of our anger.

Say what you need to say, but with truth and grace—and learn to balance the two. Ninety percent of what you communicate in your relationships is easy; it's the other ten percent that is difficult. It is the sign of a seasoned saint when you can say uncomfortable truths in a graceful way.

Emotion #4: Fear

I like a mystery that keeps you on the edge of your seat, but I have a rule in our house; we never watch scary movies at night. I guess that's because I'm a chicken and want the safety of daylight! If my heart starts racing and I get too scared, I'll walk outside and play with the dog.

The best part of being afraid is being rescued from your fear. However, anxiety is the emotion in us that is usually based on things that don't yet exist, but we seem to call them into being.

The truth of the matter is that at least 90 percent of what you are afraid of is never going to happen—so you're wasting your time worryingly needlessly. But if you dwell on it long enough, you may be bringing it on yourself.

While I realize that God allowed Satan to test Job, what he said is true in the lives of millions today: *"What I feared has come upon me; what I dreaded has happened to me"* (Job 3:25 NIV).

We have the opportunity to make choices about our anxieties. In small doses, fear is a healthy emotion, but not if it is allowed to get out of hand.

This is what God's Word tells us on the subject: *"There is no fear in love. But perfect love drives out fear, because fear has to do with punishment. The one who fears is not made perfect in love"* (1 John 4:18 (NIV).

If you are struggling with the emotion of fear today, it may be because you doubt God loves you.

Fear is based on our insecurities and the low opinion we have of ourselves.

Please read the above verse again, and I want you to think of it in a different way. Since fear has to do with correction, we conclude that we *deserve* the thing that's going to happen to us because we haven't earned the love of God or another person. We're afraid we will be exposed for the fraud that we really are and worry, "Everyone's going to know the real me." So panic grips our heart. But perfect love "drives out" fear.

That's *agape* kind of love—when you know that your heavenly Father truly loves you, and that He will make a way, even when it seems impossible. You can rest in that love and not be afraid of financial crisis, sickness, or even death. Why? Because your hope is in God, whose love covers everything.

Not for one moment do I think that the Lord is ever going to abandon me. I know He will always be with me and that I will always have a place in His kingdom. His love casts out every unreasonable fear in my life.

I pray that you will apply this principle to whatever makes you uneasy or anxious. God is greater than anything you are afraid of, and He will give you the strength you need.

Who's In Charge?

When overwhelmed with the pressures and uncertainties of life, ask the Holy Spirit to help you control your emotions. Paul gave this word of caution: *"So be careful how you live. Don't live like fools, but like those who are wise. Make the most of every opportunity in these evil days. Don't act thoughtlessly, but understand what the Lord wants you to do"* (Ephesians 5:15-17 NLT).

Men, women, and young people whose lives are centered around their emotions are on their way to a life of unhappiness and misery. Without allowing the Holy Spirit to help you control your feelings, you will find something, such as an addiction, to fill that empty void in your life.

Perhaps it's time to pay attention when the Bible counsels, *"Don't be drunk with wine, because that will ruin your life. Instead, be filled with the Holy Spirit"* (Ephesians 5:18 NLT)

We medicate ourselves with food, drugs, sex, or money—you fill in the blank. We find what will placate us temporarily, what will calm us for a short period. But none of these things have the power to repair us on the inside. This is why we need the Spirit of God.

Today, thank the Lord for giving you the gift of emotions—whether happiness, sadness, anger, or fear. Each play their part in blessing others, getting to know yourself, and bringing you closer to the One who deeply loves you.

Chapter 10

Good Grief!

On the night Jesus was betrayed, the eleven remaining disciples accompanied Him to the Garden of Gethsemane, but Peter, James, and John were invited to personally pray with the Lord in His final hours.

No one should suffer alone nor face death without a friend nearby. Pain lessens its grip on the weary soul when the love of another touches the one who is hurting. A simple human touch has that kind of power. It frees a suffering soul, if only temporarily, from the torment of pain.

Gethsemane is located near the Mount of Olives, and its very name means "Oil-Press." It was a place where olives were crushed to release their distinctive scent and oil.

Perhaps that's what our suffering is all about. It is a time of pressing that rids us of the cares of this world and releases from us the essence that brings healing and light.

Pain is a close companion on life's journey that can

simultaneously be a despised enemy and a trusted friend. May we see this as a teacher or a mentor sent to offer wisdom and insight that reveals the mysteries of the universe. It paves the road to our transformation in this world and prepares us for eternal life in the next. Jesus said, *"If anyone desires to come after Me, let him deny himself, and take up his cross, and follow Me"* (Matthew 16:24).

Each man or woman will determine to what extent he or she will embrace the call to discipleship. Some seize it with reckless abandon while others approach it like a precarious experiment. But self-denial leads to spiritual awakening—and death to self is the key to new life.

"The Passion"

The loss of life is the ultimate enemy, for each person will be struck by its icy fist and then one day be leveled with a final blow. Death seems so terminal, so hopeless, but to the believer it isn't. Christ destroyed our enemy by facing it head on.

It all began when the Creator entered His creation and became a Man. He fully embraced the human experience and clothed Himself in flesh and lived like one of us. He was born in agony, lived in suffering, and tasted death—and even the grave.

In the three decades God's Son walked the earth, He certainly felt the joys of life, such as friendship and laughter, food and sleep, travel and conversation, plus the comfort of family and a hometown. He was human in every sense of the word, but the crowning achievement of His life was what He accomplished in His agony, suffering, and pain.

In Christendom we call this period "The Passion." He didn't retreat or even surrender, but He accepted it completely and poured Himself out. He took upon His shoulders the pain of mankind and thus identified with the lowly, hurting, sick, sinful, and the seemingly forgotten.

Interestingly, several times during the final week of Christ's life on earth, He mentioned to those around Him how He would prefer to avoid the pain. To the three disciples He took to pray in the Garden of Gethsemane, they could no doubt hear Him cry out, *"Father, if you are willing, take this cup from me"* (Luke 22:42 NIV).

It was there, before His arrest, *"being in agony...His sweat became like great drops of blood falling down to the ground"* (Luke 22:44).

After Christ was taken away by Roman soldiers, He was flogged so mercilessly that the skin was stripped from his back.

At the cross, the Rescuer of the human race paid the ultimate price for our ransom in the currency of His suffering. His side was pierced with a sword. Seven-inch nails were pounded into His hands and feet. The agony was *excruciating*—which literally means "out of the cross."

It was this pain that unlocked the door to our redemption, and His suffering sealed the covenant for our salvation.

After one last breath, the Creator of the Universe was laid to rest in a borrowed tomb outside the city of Jerusalem. The body of the Lord was not silenced by the punishment of the whips, the beatings of His tormentors, or even the weight of the cross, but as a result of the sin of the world that crushed the life from His chest.

That fateful Friday, God's Son suffered, bled and died. His body was wrapped in grave clothes, laid in the tomb, which was then sealed with a heavy stone. The thud of His burial echoed throughout eternity. It will always be the greatest event in human history.

On the third day the Holy Spirit did the unthinkable, the unimaginable: *"God raised him from the dead, freeing him from the agony of death, because it was impossible for death to keep its hold on him"* (Acts 2:24 NIV).

Hallelujah! The resurrection changes everything. But it was made possible by the pain Christ endured.

FROM GRIEF TO GLADNESS

Christ conquered your greatest enemy—death. Yet He allowed suffering and pain to survive, and instead of rescuing you from their affliction, He invites you to join Him in the *"fellowship of His sufferings"* (Philippians 3:10).

While the final battle against death has been secured, we are left to wrestle against human suffering all our days on earth. On life's journey, while the circumstances of our travels are unique, we share a common experience with our fellow travelers and with Christ Himself. Yes, it is a divine fellowship.

Even though you may be hurting today, your rescue is nearer than you think. These hours of pain will soon pass and you will know Christ as you've never known Him before, in *"the power of His resurrection"* (verse 10).

The Apostle Peter was addressing you when he wrote, *"Beloved, do not think it strange concerning the fiery trial which is to try you, as though some strange thing happened to you; but rejoice to the extent that you partake of Christ's sufferings, that when His glory* is revealed, you may also be glad with exceeding joy"* (1 Peter 4:12-13).

After the resurrection, when the disciples were distraught over the thought of Jesus returning to the Father, Christ assured them, *"You will grieve, but your grief will turn to joy. A woman giving birth to a child has pain because her time has come; but when her baby is born she forgets the anguish because of her joy that a child is born into the world. So with you: Now is your time of grief, but I will see you again and you will rejoice, and no one will take away your joy"* (John 16:20-22 NIV).

Now that is *good* grief!

Expect the Unexpected!

If you ever doubted that pain is an unexpected gift, look again at the life of Job. In his darkest hour, he received this counsel: *"If I were in your shoes, I'd go straight to God, I'd throw myself on the mercy of God. After all, he's famous for great and unexpected acts; there's no end to his surprises....So, what a blessing when God steps in and corrects you. Mind you, don't despise the discipline of Almighty God!"* (Job 5:8-9, 17 MSG).

What a contrast between the first and last chapters of the book of Job. After surviving this horrendous suffering, God not only restored Job's losses, *"Indeed the Lord gave Job twice as much as he had before"* (Job 42:10).

When Job's troubles struck him, he owned *"seven thousand sheep, three thousand camels, five hundred yoke of oxen, five hundred female donkeys"* (Job 1:3). But now he had *"fourteen thousand sheep, six thousand camels, one thousand yoke of oxen, and one thousand female donkeys"* (Job 42:12).

To top it off, he became the father of *"seven sons and three daughters"* (verse 13). You may say, "That's not double; he had that many children to begin with." Well, it's not over till it's over! When Job reached heaven the original seven were waiting for him, plus seven more—that's double!

No matter how deep the valley or how dark the tunnel, when the Lord intervenes, expect the unexpected. For example, Paul the Apostle, recalling how God was working in the churches of Macedonia, wrote how *"fierce troubles came down on [them], pushing them to the very limit...the pressure triggered something totally unexpected: an outpouring of pure and generous gifts"* (2 Corinthians 8:2-3,5 MSG).

The Greatest Gift

Christ's pain was God's gift to you. *"For God so loved the world that He gave His only begotten Son, that whoever believes in Him should not perish but have everlasting life"* (John 3:16).

We also know that *"the wages of sin is death, but the gift of God is eternal life in Christ Jesus our Lord"* (Romans 6:23).

If you have never given your heart to Christ, take time to do so right now. I invite you to pray this with me:

> *Dear God, I know I'm a sinner and I want Your forgiveness! I believe that Jesus died on the cross to pay the price for my sins. Please wash me clean from all sin, shame, and guilt. I invite Jesus to become the Lord of my life, to rule and reign in my heart from this day forward. Please send Your Holy Spirit to help me obey You, and to do Your will for the rest of my life. Amen.*

If you said this from a sincere heart, you are a new person in Christ and ready to spend eternity with Him in heaven, where, *"God will wipe away every tear from [your] eyes; there shall be no more death, nor sorrow, nor crying. There shall be no more pain, for the former things have passed away"* (Revelation 21:4).

It's For You!

This side of the pearly gates, pain doesn't go away until you embrace it; then it becomes a part of you, changing you in ways you never considered. It has transforming power. But if you continue to refuse it, then pain attaches itself to you in an unnatural way, weakening your character and slowly destroying your destiny.

The message of this book is wrapped up in the words of Jesus, who said: *"Don't run from suffering; embrace it. Follow me and I'll show you how. Self-help is no help at all. Self-sacrifice is the way, my way, to finding yourself, your true self"* (Matthew 16:24-25 MSG).

This unexpected gift is for you!

FOR ADDITIONAL RESOURCES OR TO
SCHEDULE THE AUTHOR FOR SPEAKING
ENGAGEMENTS, CONTACT:

DOUG MCALLISTER

TWITTER: @dougmcallister
BLOG: dougmcallister.com
EMAIL: DougMcAllister@me.com
INTERNET: journeyfellowshipchurch.com